CHANGING
SPECIAL EDUCATION

The Open University Press
Children with Special Needs Series

Editors

PHILLIP WILLIAMS
Professor and Head of the School of Education,
University College of North Wales, Bangor.

PETER YOUNG
Formerly Tutor in the education of children with
learning difficulties, Cambridge Institute of Education;
educational writer, researcher and consultant.

Both Phillip Williams and Peter Young were members
of the Warnock Committee of Enquiry into the Education
of Handicapped Children and Young People.

This is a series of short and authoritative introductions for parents, teachers, professionals and anyone concerned with children with special needs. The series will cover the range of physical, sensory, mental, emotional and behavioural difficulties, and the changing needs from infancy to adult life in the family, at school and in society. The authors have been selected for their wide experience and close professional involvement in their particular fields. All have written penetrating and practical books readily accessible to non-specialists.

Titles in the series
HELPING THE MALADJUSTED CHILD
Denis Stott
CHANGING SPECIAL EDUCATION
Wilfred K. Brennan

In press
THE EARLY YEARS
Maurice Chazan and Alice Laing

In preparation
THE TEACHER IS THE KEY
Kenneth Weber

UNDERSTANDING LEARNING DIFFICULTIES
Kathleen Devereux

Children with Special Needs

CHANGING
SPECIAL EDUCATION

Wilfred K. Brennan

THE OPEN UNIVERSITY PRESS
Milton Keynes

The Open University Press
A division of
Open University Educational Enterprises Limited
12 Cofferidge Close
Stony Stratford
Milton Keynes MK11 1BY, England

First published 1982

British Library Cataloguing in Publication Data

Brennan, Wilfred K.
    Changing special education.—(Children with special needs)
    1. Exceptional children—Education
    I. Title   II. Series
    371.9   LC3965

    ISBN 0-335-10046-5 (cased)
    ISBN 0-335-10045-7 (paper)

Typeset by
R. James Hall Typesetting and Book Production Services
and printed by Anchor Press Ltd., Tiptree.

CONTENTS

EDITORS' INTRODUCTION

Wilfred Brennan's title, *'Changing Special Education'*, is both ambitious and challenging in its deliberate ambiguity. It triggers in our minds questions such as, 'How is special education changing?', 'How *should* we change it?' and 'How *can* we change it?' Few people are better fitted to examine and to answer those questions than Wilfred Brennan. Over a long and distinguished career he has both experienced and been an instrument of change; he has pioneered progress and planned and charted future developments. After teaching in day and residential special schools, and being head of the remedial department in a secondary school, he was a tutor at the Cambridge Institute of Education to the advanced diploma course for experienced teachers of 'children with learning difficulties' — a decade before that term was adopted by the Warnock Report. He was Inspector and then Assistant Education Officer for Special Education in the Inner London Education Authority; and, as the Director of the Schools Council project on the curriculum of the slow learner, and as a writer and lecturer he is known to teachers in special education throughout the country and abroad. He has recently received the O.B.E. for his services to special education, and his latest assignment was to head a project on the application to the ILEA of the recommendations of the Warnock Report, 'Special Educational Needs'.

The Warnock Report is rightly regarded as a blueprint for progress in special education and as an immediate contribution to changing attitudes. With over 200 recommendations it is both comprehensive and far-reaching. And already, with its shift of emphasis from the handicaps to the needs of children and young people it has changed both attitudes and legislation. But blueprints and changes of attitude and emphasis alone do not meet present needs. Blueprints must be translated into laws; legislation and attitudes must become actions, provisions and resources. There is a great gulf between, on the one hand, the Warnock Report's priorities and, on the other, the provisions of the new Education Act. Wilfred Brennan shows us that gulf and the steps that must be taken if it is to be bridged.

Making better provision for handicapped children and young people, and for their parents and families, is part and parcel of making a better society; that is a collective responsibility in the best interests of us all. It is the purpose of this series to explore that subject in some detail. We are grateful to Wilfred Brennan, as the author of the first book in our series *Children with Special Needs* for setting out so clearly the problems that must be tackled, the choices before us and the decisions we must make. It is an important and exciting look at the task of translating ideas into reality. At once authoritative and down to earth, it is a handbook for action. Administrative and organisational problems are faced as squarely as controversial issues such as integration or mainstreaming and the roles of special schools. For parents, teachers, social workers and the members of voluntary and support agencies as much as for administrators, members of multi-disciplinary teams or governing bodies and everyone interested in making a better future for those with special educational needs, Wilfred Brennan has written a practical guide. He has written with clarity and insight born of experience and deep concern. As a result he communicates both the salient features of the route we must travel and the enthusiasm and conviction we must have if we are to arrive.

Phillip Williams
Peter Young

1

WHAT ARE SPECIAL EDUCATIONAL NEEDS?

ALL CHILDREN ARE SPECIAL

Every human being is an individual and each individual is unique. Even identical twins cannot occupy the same position in space and from the beginning they each perceive their world slightly differently. In addition, other people do not interact with or react to them in exactly the same way. As a consequence of this each twin has different experience. This affects their perception, so that in growing to adulthood they develop their own personalities, shape their own knowledge and acquire their own skills; they remain close as individuals but the quality of uniqueness persists. Should they be separated in childhood they will each be affected by the environment, social and physical, in which they grow up. For most children genetic differences are added to by the same social and environmental differences noted for the twins so that divergence among individuals is greater and the quality of uniqueness more marked.

But the unique individuals are not isolated or separated. Though we are each our own person there is part of us that we share with others. Hence, though perceptions are different they have aspects which are common; though the meaning of words is personal to each, the common, shared meaning allows us to use language to communicate, and though family and neighbourhood cultures differ, common elements generate a sense of wider community which to some degree extends beyond social class, national, regional and family differences.

Teachers in classrooms cannot escape from the duality of children as individuals and as members of a group. They teach in a manner which is calculated to meet the needs of most of the group, but they know that each child will react in his or her own way, that levels of interest and motivation will differ in the group, and that individuals will exhibit different learning problems as the lesson proceeds. Some of the differences that emerge will be relatively unimportant in the classroom because they do not affect learning. Others derive their importance entirely from the fact that they *do* affect learning. It is these circumstances which interfere with learning that loom large in the classroom and the same circumstances may prescribe or restrict the informal learning in home and neighbourhood which forms part of the child's total educational experience. In the widest sense it may be said that these individual differences give rise to special educational needs and it is part of the teacher's task to identify them and to plan to meet them. The degree to which teachers do this depends upon their sensitivity to children and the level of their professional competence. Nevertheless, many individual learning needs are successfully dealt with by teachers without stress and within the constraints of the classroom and the teacher's skill. Meeting needs at this level is not usually regarded as special education and discussion of them is usually regarded as discussion of individual differences. The term *special educational needs* is reserved for more serious or multiple needs which require more than the unsupported action of the classroom teacher. It is these needs in children, wide and varied as they are, which we will now examine.

SPECIAL EDUCATIONAL NEEDS

Special educational needs do not exist in the abstract, though it is dangerously easy to discuss them in that manner. A special educational need *always* involves a child or a young person and the immediate family as well as, in some circumstances, relatives, friends, neighbours and the professional workers involved in meeting the needs of the child in school and in the family. It is very important to keep this in mind, particularly in a discussion such as this which must inevitably rest on classification, and the generalization it entails. It may assist, therefore, to start by considering some children with special educational needs.

Barry

At 13 Barry is a good looking, freckle-faced boy with blond hair and a thin angular body. At first he appears a normal teenager. But he talks a lot and one realizes that the flow is difficult to stop. And his body never stops moving. Limbs assume a continuous sequence of new postures and the eyes are equally mobile, rarely fixing on the listener. In his flow of conversation factual reality is constantly shifted in a disturbingly egocentric manner, or subjects are changed through associations almost devoid of discernible logic. Conversing with him is demanding for the adult in a manner exceeded only by the exhaustion of attempting to keep him to one subject. In fact, Barry is grossly retarded in attainment though within normal limits of intellectual ability. His hyperactivity has proved uncontainable in an ordinary classroom and his mere presence constitutes an obstacle to learning for other pupils through the disturbance he generates and his excessive demand (or need) for the attention of the teacher.

In a small, special class, carefully structured and controlled by an experienced teacher, Barry is beginning to progress in learning and shows some signs of bringing his behaviour under control. But it is difficult to imagine how he will accommodate to any of the work situations open to him on leaving school.

Molly

Conversation with Molly is as exhausting as with Barry, but for quite different reasons. She is small and slightly built for her 11 years with dark hair and deep brown eyes. But the eyes are usually downcast and when she looks at you it is with eyes upturned from a head inclined forward. She offers no word on her own initiative and even appears not to hear what is said to her. When she does respond it is usually with one word, little above a whisper as though the sound of her own voice might shatter the stillness of her personality. Molly's level of learning in reading and number is satisfactory and compatible with her intellectual level as tested, though doubts have been expressed about the result which may well have been influenced by her unforthcomingness. But there is no doubt about the inadequacy of her social learning and her failure to respond to other people in normal situations, while her reticence makes it extremely difficult to assess her actual language competence. Molly has a depressed mother and a physical, overbearing father who, it is suspected, subjected the child to ill-treatment in her early years. Social workers are concerned about the family situation but it is proving difficult to do anything positive about it.

To rehabilitate Molly successfully will require social services intervention and some changes in family relationships, but the school has an equally important task. The main task is to make Molly aware of other people, to assist her to become more positive about herself and to increase her self-confidence. Weekly sessions of psychotherapy at the local child guidance centre contribute to the task, supported by special emphasis in drama, art, music and movement in the school curriculum. At the same time all Molly's teachers are aware of the need to be positive in their relationships with her, supporting her developing confidence and encouraging her interaction with other pupils.

Jane

Jane is in a special school for maladjusted children. To see her in school one wonders why, unless one witnesses an episode. The violence of these is extreme. For practically no reason at all the normal 9-year-old explodes. No one and nothing near is safe and the physical violence and destruction are matched by the obscenity of language and gesture which punctuates the destruction. Physical restraint is necessary. The violence passes to be replaced by physical exhaustion which gradually gives way to a quiet reticence until, in a day or so, Jane becomes her usual apparently normal self—until the next outburst. The disruption in learning caused by this pattern is evidenced in Jane's backwardness as well as in her difficulty in keeping friends.

Expert teachers, psychotherapy and psychiatric supervision combine to assist and support the child but her "rehabilitation" will be a long process and her education difficult.

John

John is 17 and attends a specially-designed unit for physically handicapped pupils in a comprehensive school. Bright and cheerful, with a good word for all his teachers and school friends, he is universally liked and has responded well to the teaching offered in his school, achieving six "O" levels and hoping for two "A" levels. John's day is spent in a wheelchair for he is without legs and as his hands are appendages to rudimentary arms, he requires constant attendance to move from class to class or even around the classroom. There is no doubt about the boy's high intellectual ability which is clearly reflected in his conversation as well as by tests and by his achievements. John is a splendid example of what may be achieved by special education wherever it is given.

Robert

Robert is in a special school for physically handicapped children.
At first his handicap seems mild compared with John's for his
body is well proportioned and normal for his 12 years. When he
moves there is some slight lack of coordination and his "reach to
grasp" is somewhat haphazard; yet these are mild conditions
hardly justifying his presence in a special school. It is in school
work that Robert's handicap becomes obvious. His handwriting is
ill-formed, irregular, unevenly spaced and practically unreadable;
his reading is equally retarded, hesitant, with words missed and
frequent regressions along lines notwithstanding his word by word
attack on the print; and his apparent inability to align figures on a
page proves a major obstacle in his number work. Manual skills
exhibit a similar lack of precision and a complete inability to work
to fine limits at the level achieved by Robert's age-mates. Yet in
conversation, apart from a slight slurring of words, Robert appears
more at the level of his age in both interests and ability though
with occasional illogical association of subjects and some misunderstanding due to lapses of attention. The latter are usually due to
easy distraction by any sensory stimuli impinging on the situation,
a feature noted by teachers in Robert's classroom behaviour.

Altogether, the picture is typical of many physically handicapped children. The mild physical disability has little effect on
learning but serious learning problems arise from associated
disabilities in the nervous system which affect perception, attention and fine motor control. The difficulties faced by pupils like
Robert are easily underestimated.

Kathleen

Kathleen is lying on the floor of her classroom supported by soft
cushions, surrounded by suspended "mobiles" amid music which
it is doubtful if she can hear. Without the cushions her body would
have flopped like a rag doll, resting where it lay until some other
person or force moved it. She has no speech and it is thought she
can hear nothing but the loudest shout. Dressing and feeding are
beyond her and only possible through loving, caring parents at
home assisted by equally caring staff at her special school. So far
as is known, Kathleen is severely mentally handicapped with
central nervous system impairment resulting in almost complete
physical dependence on other people; she has no speech and little
sensory perception, though the teacher and welfare workers who

care for her claim that there is some communication in the slight changes of expression which flit across her face from time to time. Her parents support this view and say she shows awareness when other members of the family enter a room. But to a stranger this communication does not exist.

Here is a girl of 18 years at a total dependancy level near that of a new-born infant. Kathleen shares the "special care" which her school offers with six other children and young people with similar, severe levels of disability.

Bertie

This young man is in the same school as Kathleen but in the ordinary classes. He is a happy, talkative 14-year-old, stubby and overweight, with a shock of blond hair and the wide face, slanting eyes and protruding tongue of a child with Down's syndrome, often referred to as "mongolism". A closer look reveals the flattened skull, short, broad hands and roughened skin often associated with these children. Bertie is mentally handicapped but not at the extremely severe level of Kathleen. He reads a few common words, counts with a degree of accuracy to about ten and knows the common coins and their approximate value. He feeds and dresses himself in an acceptable manner, though more slowly than a normal boy of his age. Bertie's language is at about the normal seven-year-old level though he uses some words which are above that level and to other words he gives a unique, personal meaning which might be found among others in his school. Within a situation with which he is familiar, this young man behaves with considerable confidence and assurance.

Bertie has been brought to his present level through patient and careful teaching. He had to be taught many things which most children learn for themselves, so his curriculum and teaching made great demands on the staff of his school. Learning had to be presented in small steps which he could master, each carefully designed to keep him motivated, and each small success requiring immediate reward and continual repetition and reinforcement.

Anne

Anne is blind. Educationally that does not mean that she has no sight, but that she must be educated by methods which do not make use of sight. She does, in fact, perceive a shadow world and her school makes maximum use of this in training her to find her way around the environment. Otherwise use is made of her other senses to compensate for her lack of visual perception. She reads and writes braille through a series of raised dots representing an alphabet discerned through her finger tips. Anne has potentially normal learning ability and is expected to progress to normal levels of secondary education though the goals will be achieved later than by her non-handicapped peers.

Not all the blind children in her special school will make the same progress for some have intellectual and other limitations which would handicap their learning even if they had sight. Some children with very poor sight can nevertheless use it in learning and would be educated as partially-sighted children. However, it is often difficult to decide whether to educate these children as blind or partially sighted.

Donald

Donald has grave difficulty in hearing and what he does hear is so distorted that it is next to useless as a means of communication. Indeed, it is doubtful if his hearing could meet the elementary task of offering him some safeguard against approaching danger. Hearing aids do not help him. They tend to magnify the distortions and elevate what he may just hear to a level that is uncomfortable or even unbearable. Donald is 4 and is learning to "talk". The specially-trained teacher in his special school takes infinite care over the task, making sure that Donald closely observes her face, lips and tongue, touches them, feels their movement, and becomes aware of her breath on his face with attention to its pattern and force. The little boy attempts to replicate his teacher's formulation of a word. He observes her face and feels it; then does the same using a mirror to see his own. To a normally hearing person the patience required by teacher and pupil is painful and the same word could be applied to progress, for after many years the pupil's speech may mean little except to those in close contact with him. Opinion and practice differ among teachers of deaf children about how much use should be made of signing systems (sign language) and, if used, which system should be employed.

It is difficult to say where Donald's educational future will be. He is believed to be well above average in intellectual ability so he will, therefore, almost certainly learn to use lip reading as means of communication and, if his hearing allows it, his teachers will make use of highly sophisticated electronic aids to establish the intercommunication upon which education depends. Donald could achieve the goals of normal secondary education. If he does it will be through the support of expert and dedicated specialist teachers of deaf children — right from the start.

Not all the pupils in Donald's school have his level of ability and there will be those who, if they were not deaf, might require education as backward pupils and others who may be maladjusted. There are some children who through the use of hearing aids can be educated as partially hearing pupils in ordinary schools, supported by a unit for the partially hearing.

David

David is in the top bracket of intellectual ability with an Intelligence Quotient consistently around the 140 mark. He is alert, knowledgeable beyond his 13 years, a regular viewer of Open University TV programmes about which he can converse with intelligence and insight, especially in scientific matters. He has wide-ranging hobbies including rock and butterfly collecting, tropical fish, gardening and greenhouse management. Yet he finds it difficult to maintain a place in the middle of a second-year class at second intellectual level in his comprehensive school. His trouble is that though he understands the tasks set and knows how to complete them correctly, he just cannot put his work on paper in the time allowed in class and his spelling is atrocious. Homework tasks follow the same pattern. A half-hour exercise for a normal pupil becomes two hours of grind for David, with all the frustration that this entails for a boy who knows exactly what is required. The finished work, though grossly immature in presentation, is equally sophisticated in content—but there is always a backlog of work devouring time.

David is receiving remedial education to counter his perceptual and fine motor difficulties even though little is known about them. Otherwise, he is being educated normally.

George

George belongs to a group of children forming the most extensive kind of educational disability. He is not mentally handicapped but his intellectual ability is such that he has great difficulty in coping with normal school learning, especially in reading, writing and arithmetic. He comes from a home which meets most of his emotional needs but falls short in the model of language that it presents to him and fails to provide the intellectual stimulation and broad experience necessary if pupils are to make maximum use of the education offered in school. Consequently George needs to learn in school many things which teachers usually take for granted and, equally, the school must provide experience and associated language which is required as a basis for George's education. This boy belongs to the wide group of pupils for long referred to as *educationally subnormal* officially, or as backward, retarded or slow learners in the shorthand of the school. Fortunately George is a stable adolescent and maintains good relationships with his teachers and his peers.

If he is to become an adult adequately meeting the personal, social and economic demands made on him, he needs an appropriate curriculum, well taught, in a situation which allows the close individual attention from the teacher that he requires for success. George's level of intellectual limitation is to be found in most special schools for children with other handicaps.

Susan

In the current terminology Susan is a "delicate" pupil. She has a mild, congenital heart condition and a long history of chest infections which have involved frequent absence from school.

When in school Susan learns normally but is retarded because her education has been subject to much interruption. It was thought that the stress of her ordinary school was a factor in her frequent infections and that a quieter, more supportive regime would be beneficial to her education as well as to her physical condition. This proved correct. Infection and associated absence have been reduced since she entered her special school and if the improvement continues she may be able to enter a special class for delicate children when she enters secondary school in two years' time with, perhaps, later placement in the ordinary classes of the school.

Susan, and indeed most of the children described above, may have spent time in hospital or may, for various reasons, have had to remain at home rather than attend any school. Hospital schools and visiting teachers (usually designated as the Home Tuition Service) provide for the children's needs in these circumstances.

The above descriptions illustrate the variety of conditions which give rise to special educational needs though they by no means include all those faced by teachers in special and ordinary schools. But they do reinforce the point that there is always a child or young person involved whenever there is a special need.

DISABILITY AND HANDICAP

There is no clear, agreed definition of the differences between terms such as handicap, disability, incapacity and disadvantage; a circumstance which introduces uncertainty in many discussions. This situation is not assisted by the fact that, whatever the term used, the individual considered is unlikely to be affected by it over the whole range of his behaviour. It has already been noted that not all the differences which emerge in classrooms affect the education of the pupils and the same is true of significant differences to which the term disability might be applied. In the descriptions of handicapped children, for instance, only Kathleen is handicapped in a manner which may affect all her behaviour; John has serious physical disabilities which will certainly affect his participation in sport and restrict his employment possibilities, but his educational achievement would be considered highly satisfactory even in the absence of his physical disabilities; and David, though unable to realize his intellectual potential in school, is involved in rich and extensive intellectual and practical activities where his disability in writing is no handicap. George has a disability which will be a handicap to learning all through school and the probability is that his educational attainments on leaving school will be restricted even if he is taught appropriately and efficiently. But when he leaves school he will leave behind the greater part of his handicap, for boys like George merge easily into the level of economic and social activities which are typical of large sections of the workers in our industrialized society. Susan presents another interesting circumstance. Her disability certainly appeared as a handicap in her ordinary school where she failed to make progress, yet in her special school the handicap was reduced and is likely to disappear in time. Throughout this change the inner condition which generated the disability remained unchanged but the change in external circumstances reduced the associated handicap. Donald and Anne both have serious disabilities which reduce to a minimum the operation of major sensory contact with the environment, and little can be done to alter this circumstance. Handicap here is almost total so far as the affected senses are concerned, though there may be some compensation through intact sensory channels. How far the disability becomes a handicap for Donald and Anne may depend on the level and patterns of their aspirations and the degree to which these require the functions of hearing for Donald or sight for Anne. For Barry, Molly and Jane the effect of their disabilities on formal school learning may be of less account than the effect on their relationships with other people. The outside world will not adjust to these children as their schools have done. Unless they achieve a degree of stability before young adulthood the tensions they will generate for others will constitute a real handicap in workplace, in social situations and in intimate personal relationships.

From the above discussion *disability* may be regarded as a loss of capacity or function due to physical, sensory, neurological, intellectual or emotional impairment. The cause of the disability may often be determined (though not necessarily rectified) and it may also be possible to measure or assess the degree of impairment in relation to what is considered to be normal. Whether or not the disability constitutes a *handicap* is more difficult to determine and hazardous to predict for it depends on many variables. Certain disabilities handicap individuals in some situations but not in others, or for a specific period during the individuals's life. Many scholastic handicaps have this pattern. Family aspirations may create a handicap if there is insistence that the child should endeavour to succeed in an area where his disability is an obstacle to progress. The pupil's own aspirations may have a similar effect where physical disability is allied to a desire for sporting success or intellectual limitation to scholastic achievement. Disability also relates to career goals. Railway drivers and guards need normal colour vision but this may not be important for the booking office clerk; jobs requiring physical strength, stamina or accuracy of movement may be unsuitable for persons with a physical disability, or even for some persons with ill-health, but there are many jobs which do not require these attributes where their disability does not constitute a handicap. An important part of the education of children with disabilities consists of helping them to come to terms with their disabilities in the sense that they are able to shape their goals and aspirations towards areas where the disability is not a handicap and so obtain that measure of success which each individual needs for healthy living.

AGE, DEVELOPMENT AND SPECIAL NEEDS

As children grow older they usually become bigger, heavier, stronger, understand and use more words, generate more complex sentences, become more competent socially and (most of them) better socially adjusted as self-regulation is established. It is easily overlooked that this also occurs for children with disabilities. The individual child's disability may remain unaltered but the child grows, develops and *changes*. Consequently the effect of a disability may change, in particular the degree to which it constitutes a handicap for the child. Put another way, it must not be overlooked that, even if special needs are permanent, those needs will change as the individual grows and develops. In some sad cases, such as the children with muscular dystrophies, there may be progressive degeneration of the disability leading to an increase in handicap so far as physical activity is concerned, though intellectual development may be unimpaired. For other children planned medical or surgical intervention may change the disabling condition, reduce impairment and consequently reduce or eliminate handicap in ways which may have significant consequences for their education and life prospects.

Apart from the changes in the individual child, situations may be altered through changes in the environment. Improved quality of social service support for child and family may open new prospects for education. Developments to allow the education of handicapped children in ordinary schools, or improved staffing and facilities in special schools, may lead to revision of educational plans. The introduction of new industries into a locality may open new career opportunities and these may be enhanced by an extension of the provision for pupils with disabilities to become students in Colleges of Further Education. But these circumstances, too, may operate in reverse. Lowering of economic activity may reduce employment prospects for the handicapped more than for normal workers. Cuts in social services or education may reduce the quality of care and education and inequitable allocation or mismanagement in local government may have the same effect.

It follows that any initial assessment of special needs is not of itself sufficient. It must be supported by a regular and consistent review of the disabilities of individual children and their careful evaluation in terms of changing environmental circumstances and the life prospects of the child.

CATEGORIES OF HANDICAPPED PUPILS

The last decade of the nineteenth century saw the beginning of recognition and provision for pupils with marked disabilities in the growing public educational system. The growth of provision has been documented by Pritchard (1963)[1] and summarized in

Chapter 2 of the *Warnock Report* (1978)[2] but each extension was marked by a concentration on the *categorization* of the handicapping conditions to be provided for. Though necessary for legal definitions, the approach has had an unfortunate effect in encouraging the categorization of educational thinking. Thus, prior to 1944, Local Education Authorities (LEAs) had a duty to provide special education for blind, deaf, physically defective, epileptic and mentally defective children. The Education Act 1944 extended the duties of LEAs to securing provision, in special schools or otherwise, for children suffering from a disability of mind or body. The Secretary of State for Education was required to make regulations defining the *categories* of pupils in need of *special educational treatment* so that, welcome though the extension was, it continued the emphasis on categories and added the concept of *treatment* which put special education into a disease framework more suited to the practice of medicine than the process of education.

Regulations defining the categories of handicapped pupils have been revised since 1944. At present there are ten categories: blind, partially sighted, deaf, partially-hearing, delicate, education-ally subnormal, epileptic, maladjusted, physically handicapped and children with speech defects, all legally defined by the *Handicapped Pupils and Special School Regulations*, (1959)[3] as reproduced in Appendix 1. In addition the Education (Handicapped Children) Act 1970 made LEAs responsible for the education of severely mentally handicapped children previously considered unsuitable for education in school and they were included as a sub-category; educationally subnormal (severe). In the same year the Chronically Sick and Disabled Persons Act (1970) required LEAs to make arrangements for the education of children who were both blind and deaf, for those suffering from autism and other forms of childhood psychosis, and for children with acute dyslexia.

It is interesting to note that the recent additional categories, ESN (severe), blind/deaf, autistic and dyslexic have not been brought into the close legal definitions of *Handicapped Pupils and Special School Regulations*. Possibly this was because of mounting criticism of the rigidity of the regulations and a growing belief that they were an obstacle to the development of special education, culminating in the broader concept of special educational needs to be discussed in Chapter 4. But there had been other changes. Over the years the pattern of defined categories of handicap changed as the virtual disappearance of tuberculosis and poliomyelitis reduced the number of physically handicapped and delicate pupils and the number of blind children also declined, though there was an increase in the number of educationally subnormal and maladjusted pupils. The number with spina bifida, a crippling condition, rose for a time but appears to have levelled off. But most marked over the years has been the increase in the incidence of children suffering from multiple handicaps which present great problems in assessment and even greater problems for the teachers who must educate the children. The rigidity of the legal definitions and the special schools organized in accordance with them made it exceptionally difficult to make proper provision for multiply handicapped children and directed attention to the limitations of a system so organized. This is not to say that the categories served no purpose, for they did direct attention to the handicapped children and provided impetus to the development of special education. But as the system developed, as knowledge and experience increased, the inherent limitations of the system became more and more obvious. And the system of special education was growing. At ten-year intervals the total number of handicapped pupils in special schools increased as follows: 1945 — 38,499; 1955 — 58,034; 1965 - - 70,334, 1975 — 122,268. (DES 1979)[4].

By 1977 there were 135,261 pupils in special schools distributed among the categories of handicap as:

Blind	1,255
Partially sighted	2,205
Deaf	3,627
Partially hearing	2,111
Physically handicapped	13,083
Delicate	4,404
Maladjusted	13,687
Educationally subnormal:	
medium	55,698
severe	22,839
Epileptic	2,096
Speech defect	4,715
Autistic	562
In hospital schools	8,979

Of these pupils 61% were boys, 39% girls. The age distribution is also of interest in comparison with the local example below.

Table 1.1   *Age-group distribution of children in special schools in 1977*

Age group by years	Under 5	5—11	12—16	Over 16
Per cent of pupils	3	45	30	1.41

Boarding schools provided residential education for 21,184 pupils forming 16% of the total of handicapped children in schools (DES 1979)[5] . On waiting lists for admission to special schools there were 6,716 children, and 21,674 handicapped pupils were attending designated special classes in ordinary schools; 5,798 children were being educated other than in school. The 169,449 handicapped pupils noted above formed 1.75% of the 9,663,978 pupils in all types of schools. The cost of special education was £234.4 million or 9.7% of expenditure on schools.

The growth and extent of provision for handicapped pupils may be more meaningful if placed within the context of one LEA, again using the current catagories of handicapped pupils.

A LOCAL EXAMPLE

The situation described here is not put forward as typical. It represents a variety of provision for handicapped children achieved in a major English education authority with a long and distinguished history in the development of special education for handicapped children. At the time of writing there were 9,307 pupils in special schools, including 478 pupils from other LEAs and they formed 2.65% of the total schools population between the ages of 2 and 19 years. Their age distribution was as follows

Table 1.2   *Age-group distribution of 9,307 pupils in special schools in one LEA*

Age group by years	2—4	5—10	11—16	17—19
Per cent of pupils	3.1	30.4	64.7	1.7

It will be noted that the distribution departs from that of the national figures given above. In fact, pupils between 5 and 10 years formed only 1.89% of the total age range in contrast with the 11--16 group where handicapped pupils amounted to 3.69% of the group.

In addition to the above pupils, 451 handicapped pupils were placed in schools outside the authority; 337 were waiting for special school placement. Another group of handicapped pupils was receiving education in ordinary schools: 365 in units for partially hearing pupils; 715 in tutorial classes for maladjusted pupils; and 350 in remedial classes for backward pupils. Apart from these designated situations, nurture groups in primary schools, sanctuaries in secondary schools, remedial arrangements in both types of school and educational guidance centres for unsettled secondary pupils provided for a transient population of pupils with less serious difficulties. Variety is also reflected in the schools and units provided in the authority. There were 84 day and 32 boarding special schools; 6 hospital schools; 15 units for partially hearing pupils in ordinary schools; 38 tutorial classes; 28 remedial classes; 34 groups under section 56 of the Education Act 1944; 1 school and 30 groups in social service establishments; 8 home tuition centres; 2 structured classes for maladjusted pupils; 2 classes for pupils with perceptual difficulties; 6 classes for pupils with language disorder or delay; 10 educational guidance units; and 6 hostels for pupils attending day special schools.

Handicapped pupils were distributed over the schools and units as follows:

Table 1.3   Distribution of pupils in special schools and classes

	Per cent in special schools	Per cent in special classes
ESN(M)	36.9	
ESN(S)	15.3	
Delicate	14.3	
Maladjusted	13.4	50.0
Physically handicapped	6.0	
Partially sighted	3.9	
Deaf	2.2	
Blind	0.9	
Partially hearing	0.9	24.5
Autistic	0.7	
Physical handicap + other handicap	0.7	
In hospital schools	3.9	
In remedial classes	-	25.5

A point to note from the Table 1.3 is that in this LEA there is no alternative to a special school for most of the handicaps. On the other hand, the special school for partially hearing pupils is a boarding school and there is no alternative to the special classes on a day-school basis.

In its special schools the authority employed 1,712 teachers, 431 child care staff, 214 nursery assistants, 7 media resources staff and 1,247 other workers. The total cost of operating special schools in the year quoted was £31,200,000 net or 9.9% of the expenditure on schools.

EACH UNIT IS A CHILD

The national and local situations demonstrate the growth and extent of education for handicapped pupils but it must not be overlooked that each unit figure represents a child, and beyond the child a family facing problems which are not experienced by the great majority of people in the community.

In the same way, each unit figure for a school or unit represents a concerned group of workers, professional and others supported by psychological, social and medical colleagues. And beyond them the clerical and administrative workers who maintain the system of special education providing the schools and resources which make it possible for those in the schools to carry out their task. Legally responsible for the whole complex are the elected members of the Local Education Authority, in particular those members who serve on the sub-committee responsible for special education. The cost of the special education is met from money raised locally through the rates and grants from the central government. But the focal point and justification for all this is the handicapped child and the purpose is to provide special education that is appropriate, efficient and compassionate.

SUMMARY

An attempt has been made to show that all children are special in that each has the quality of uniqueness. Yet each child has something in common with others and can interact with them in a group. Teachers must take account of children as individuals and as membes of a class group, the latter in the presentation of learning situations and the former through taking account of individual differences. Some differences do not affect the child's learning but those which do assume importance for the teacher. There are differences which are more than an individual teacher can cope with in the classroom and these are referred to as "special educational needs". Thinking about the needs was for long influenced by the designation of categories of handicapped children and the special schools were developed to accord with the categories. Changes in incidence of handicaps and the recognition of new handicaps put a strain on the system. But it was the increased incidence of multiply-handicapped children, difficult to place in the system, which more than anything directed attention to the inadequacy of legal definitions for educational handicap. Examples have been given of the growth of special educational provision nationally, in terms of the total number of handicapped children, and of the variety of provision through the number of pupils in each handicapped category. An example from a local education authority illustrated the problem at local level, and indicated the provision made for special education.

Throughout the discussion emphasis has been placed on the individual children behind the generalizations and these have been illustrated through case sketches. The difference between *disability* as a reduction or impairment of function and *handicap* as a barrier to a goal or objective desired by the individual has been brought out. It was seen that handicap was the more difficult to assess because of the many variables to be taken into account. Also emphasized was the fact that few disabilities generate all-round handicap, in the usual situation handicap is restricted to specific circumstances or activities. Many scholastic handicaps do not operate outside schools and some severe handicaps do not affect education. The point has been made that the effect of a disability may change as the child grows and develops, as a result of medical or surgical intervention or as a result of changes in the environment in which the child lives. These changes may improve the child's life prospects or, in some circumstances, have a detrimental effect on them. Because of this, the initial assessment must be supported by regular review and evaluation of the child's educational and life prospects.

NOTES AND REFERENCES

1 PRITCHARD, D.G. (1963) *Education and the Handicapped*, Routledge and Kegan Paul.

2 DEPARTMENT OF EDUCATION AND SCIENCE (1978), *Special Educational Needs*, HMSO.

3 DEPARTMENT OF EDUCATION AND SCIENCE (1959), *Handicapped Pupils and Special Schools*. Regulations as amended 1962, HMSO.

4 Department of Education and Science (1979) Statistics of Education, Vol. I, 1977. H.M.S.O.

2

DISCOVERING AND ASSESSING
SPECIAL EDUCATIONAL NEEDS

THE PEOPLE CONCERNED

The discovery and assessment of special educational needs involves
many people and it may be useful to list them before discussing
the process itself.

Parents

Parents are the persons closest to their own child and in the natural
and legal sense it is they who are responsible for the child. In
normal circumstances, the intimacy of parenthood gives them
access to information and insights about the child's needs which
cannot be obtained from any other source. It is of the first importance, therefore, that parents are closely involved in the assessment
of their child's special needs—from the start and throughout the
process. Passive acquiescence is not sufficient: what is required is
active cooperation to the full extent allowed by other family
demands which the parents must meet. In this kind of relationship
professional workers learn much from parents, but for parents
also the process is a learning experience. From the experience
parents gain a deeper and broader understanding of the educational
aspects of their child's special needs, including the proposals
eventually made for special education. More important, they are
able to evaluate the proposals in a realistic manner. This desirable
level of parental involvement is not always achieved at present,
and, in particular, there is often failure to involve parents when a
child in ordinary school first encounters significant learning

difficulties; many subsequent difficulties may be traced back to these circumstances.

In many instances it is anxious parents who first direct attention to the fact that their child is not making progress. They may do this through the health visitor, the family doctor or the teacher if the child is in school. Otherwise it may be a professional worker who suspects special needs and faces the problem of alerting or informing parents. Whatever the circumstances the parents will require sensitive support which takes account of their natural anxiety, and this is more likely to be successful where parents are made aware that they are full and welcome partners in the investigation of their child's special needs as well as important participants in his or her special education.

Hospital staff

Many severe handicaps are diagnosed at birth, and the doctors and nurses involved must make the decision as to when and how the parents are to be told. If the condition is not obvious to the mother they may delay until they have consulted the family doctor and in some circumstances it may fall to him to inform the parents. Where there is doubt a medical consultant with a relevant background may see the child, and his advice may determine when and how the parents should be informed. These decisions are not easy. A natural first question from a mother is "Is she all right?" and the answer requires sensitivity if she is not and diplomacy also where there is doubt. In the cases where there is obvious disability at birth the process of counselling and supporting the mother must begin in hospital. Fathers too must be involved and at an early stage, for the child is born into the family.

Family doctor

Whether or not the family doctor has been involved in the hospital he will certainly come into the situation when mother returns home with a handicapped child. Often he will have to deal with parents who are both upset and insecure, anxious for information, needing support and reassurance. Where signs of possible disability emerge in the first weeks or months of life the family doctor will be in a position similar to that of the hospital staff described above. He may have to refer the child to a consultant and take the decision about how the parents are to be informed.

Health visitor

The health visitor is employed by the local health district. She is a qualified nurse trained and experienced in work with infants and young children; she will make statutory visits to all mothers with new-born infants, extend the visits as required, and become the link between the mother, the local health services and clinics and the family doctor. It may, indeed, be the health visitor who first becomes aware of the possibility of special needs in the child, and to her may fall the major task of support for the mother. Where there is a long period of investigation the mother may have a special need for support from the health visitor.

Social worker

The social worker is employed by the Social Service department of the local council. Hers is not a medical service but she will be able to offer further support to the mother. Most often she will have been called in through the health visitor if not already supporting the family. Through the social worker the family may receive practical support, income where necessary, alterations to the house to accommodate the child's needs, contact with other parents of similar children, and an introduction to voluntary associations concerned with the families of handicapped children. The involvement of the social worker and her department will continue as long as it is necessary for the family; but the service is voluntary and it will be regulated also by the willingness of the parents to accept it.

Voluntary societies

Voluntary societies usually concern themselves with one type or range of handicap and their concern may extend from birth to the end of life. Some, such as those working with blind or deaf children, employ full-time social workers who are often well informed and experienced in the special needs of young children. Such workers are not usually involved in the discovery of special needs but their contributions may be especially valuable in the assessment of need. Otherwise the role of the societies is mainly a supportive one for the family and child though they are, in some circumstances, able to bring useful pressure to bear on central government, local authorities and the health services and this contributes to improvement in the quality of discovery and assessment.

Educational welfare officers

The Educational welfare officers (EWO) are employed by the local education authorities. They have a wide range of duties and are unlikely to be involved with children under 2 years of age, the weight of their work being with children over 5. It is with children whose special needs first attract attention in school that EWOs become involved. Their work overlaps that of the social worker and where she is involved with a family regular consultation may be necessary to avoid duplication of function. Either the EWO or the social worker may contribute information about family background and circumstances to the assessment process and the question may need careful determination where both are involved. With most families there will be no social service involvement and the EWO will become the link with the LEA and the main contributor of social information in the assessment process.

Peripatetic pre-school teachers

The organization of peripatetic pre-school teaching varies between local education authorities and in some areas may not be provided. Where it is, it is usually confined to work with pre-school children who are deaf or blind or mentally handicapped (ESN severe). The teachers will have training and experience in the handicap with which they are concerned as well as experience with young children. They work on the basis of home visits and their role is to stimulate and teach the handicapped child, in the process teaching the mother so that she, too, becomes involved in the task with her own child. The teacher, because of her background, will be able to keep the mother informed about the schools and educational services available for her child. It is important that the teacher maintains good, close liaison with the health visitor and/or social worker and does not usurp their role but, rather, works through them where necessary. These specialized teachers should be involved in providing educational information when the children are assessed or reviewed and they should be called in whenever their specialized knowledge can contribute to the assessment of a child.

Educational psychologists

Educational psychologists are employed by the local education authorities. It is usual for an educational psychologist to have an honours degree in psychology followed by one year of teacher training, two years of teaching experience and one year of training in educational psychology. Using her knowledge of child development and her skill in testing and assessment, the psychologist prepares reports on the psychological aspects of the child's special needs which should be helpful both in assessment and in decisions about the kind of special education necessary to meet the child's needs. She may also be a source of advice for teachers and parents where children exhibit complex learning or behaviour difficulties.

Inspectors/Advisers in special education

The designation as inspector or adviser differs among the LEAs which employ them. Whatever the title they are qualified teachers with substantial experience in ordinary schools as well as with handicapped children. Usually they have had advanced training in special education at the level of a university diploma or degree. Practice varies, but inspectors/advisers tend to have a remit over the range of handicaps together with specialization in certain areas of special need. Their first task is to supervise the work of teachers and the quality of education in special schools, special classes, or with handicapped pupils wherever they may be educated. As part of this work they organize the in-service training of teachers. In addition they are responsible for the specialized advice required by the LEA to maintain the standard of special education and develop it in response to local needs. It is also part of their remit to provide specialized educational advice and support for parents, who should have direct access to them. Inspectors in special education also contribute to the assessment of special needs and advise on appropriate school placements for individual children.

Assistant Education Officers for special education

In the structure of a LEA the AEO/SE is the administrator responsible for special education, answering to the Chief Education Officer of the Authority and, through him, to the committee of the Authority which supervises special education. Executive action on committee decisions, budgeting and organization of the special education service, conduct of the service in accordance with Education Acts and other government instructions, supervision of the work in the special education branch of the LEA; all these are part of the AEO/SE responsibility. In addition, he must formulate development proposals for submission to the SE committee and, in doing this, he receives professional advice from SE inspectors, educational psychologists, the school welfare service and the school medical service. The AEO/SE also has a role with parents. Any parents who are not satisfied with the education being offered to their child, and are not reassured by other advisers in the authority, may bring their case to the AEO. Groups of parents or associations concerned with the education and welfare of handicapped children may well raise their points with the LEA through the AEO/SE.

School medical officers

School medical officers are employed by the district health services. They are responsible for the statutory examination of pupils in schools and for advice about medical aspects of the conduct of the school. They have a general supervisory role in relation to individual children which is especially important for the medical aspects of children with special needs and for their parents. It is important to understand that in this role SMOs facilitate action on medical aspects of a child's condition, they do not directly treat the condition. Within the health service organization a senior medical officer will have a specialist responsibility for offering medical advice relevant to the conduct and development of the special education service.

Medical Consultants

Where a child's special needs involve a serious medical, orthopaedic or surgical condition there is usually a consultant involved in the treatment. The specialized advice may be exercised through the family doctor and the SMO is also aware of the advice and is helpful where it has implications for the school. In special schools, where there is often a concentration of pupils with consultant involvement, a trend has developed whereby consultants hold clinics on school premises to which parents are invited. The involvement of consultants in the assessment of seriously handicapped pre-school children has been noted previously. They also contribute to assessment or reassessment of handicapped children with whom they are concerned at any age. However, with children of school age the consultant's contribution is put into the assessment process through the medical element provided by the school medical officer.

Teachers

The whole process of the assessment of special needs and the placement of children with those needs in situations appropriate to their education may be regarded as directed at making sure that the teachers who must teach and educate the children are enabled to do so appropriately and efficiently. But teachers also contribute to the assessment process, in particular for children who are attending school. They do this through the school reports which form an important part in the examination of a child who is thought to have special educational needs. All teachers in the schools of LEAs are trained and qualified for their work and the greater part of the teaching force have years of experience with children. Intimate knowledge and experience of children with special needs is concentrated into about 35% of the teaching force and approximately half of these will have additional training for their work. Almost all teachers of blind or deaf children have special training for their work as this is a legal requirement for work in these areas of disability. Each ordinary or special school has a headteacher to whom all teachers in the school are directly responsible, professionally. The headteacher is responsible for the conduct, organization and curriculum of the school in association with the school governors who are appointed by the LEA and usually include staff and parent governors. The responsibility extends to all children in the school, including those with special educational needs. In large ordinary schools direct responsibility for children with special needs may be delegated to a member of the teaching staff. Most LEAs have a policy encouraging a direct relationship between parents and teachers, which is of increased importance for parents of children with special needs. Parents should be aware of this and they have a responsibility to ensure that the schoolteachers are kept informed about the child and the child's needs. In doing this the parents should work through the headteacher of the school as this is the accepted professional procedure. The headteacher, in turn, has a responsibility to see that parents are kept informed of their child's progress in school and most headteachers will wish to foster a direct relationship between the parents and the class or subject teachers responsible for the child. It is now widely recognized that parents have an important contribution to make in the assessment of their child's needs and in his special education; good interaction between parents and teachers should facilitate this, but it also enhances the quality of the teacher's contribution to the assessment and reassessment of the child's special educational needs.

Child Guidance Clinics

A Child Guidance Clinic (a different title may be used in some areas, e.g. Family and Child Guidance Service) is the base for a team of workers concerned with children who have severe emotional difficulties, behaviour disorders or both of these combined. The team treats many children who remain in their ordinary schools, but when special education is thought to be necessary then the major input to the assessment process will come from the child guidance team. The team consists of the following members.

Psychiatrist The psychiatrist is employed by the district health authority or may be a consultant on the staff of a hospital. He is a qualified medical doctor who has taken further training in psychological medicine and is equipped to diagnose and treat mental and emotional difficulties or abnormalities. On the positive side he is able to offer advice about relations and circumstances conducive to good mental health.

The background and responsibility of the educational psychologist have been described above, and the psychologist member of the team may work in the school psychological service with some sessions of his time allocated to work in the clinic. In this role he may be directly involved in the treatment of individual children or groups of children.

Psychiatric Social Worker Not all teams have psychiatric social workers, but where they exist they are a link with the family in the home and have a special concern for the mental health aspects of family relationships as they affect the child. The psychiatric social worker may or may not have additional training for this work but she will certainly have acquired special skills as a result of her experience. The interest of the PSW also extends to the child in school, a responsibility which may overlap with the educational psychologist and any other social worker involved with the family. Good cooperation is necessary here if support is to be effective without over-intrusion on family and school.

Remedial Teacher Not all teams have such a teacher. When they have, the teacher functions as a full member of the team with special responsibility for educational aspects of treatment.

Psychotherapist Not all teams have psychotherapists. This worker is trained in techniques of working with children and using therapeutic techniques which assist children to resolve their difficulties or bring them under more direct control. It is not usual for psychotherapists to have medical training though they usually have a psychology degree and training in therapeutic methods. As a general rule, psychotherapists work under the supervision of a psychiatrist. There is some overlap between the work of the psychotherapist and the treatment side of the psychologist's work; and in the absence of the former the latter may be more deeply involved in treatment.

It may be seen from the above descriptions that many workers have a role in the process of assessing special needs. Not all will be involved with each child and the particular combination is determined by the needs and age of the child, the family circumstances and even by the source from which attention was directed to the possible existence of special needs. Although the workers may vary, their disciplines reduce to education, psychology, social work, medicine and psychiatry; and the weight of each contribution is determined by the nature of each child's disabilities. But whatever the combination, the parents play a critical role and the next common factor is the need of each child for appropriate education and teaching. The latter factor cannot be too strongly stressed. Its acceptance by all workers in assessment should assist them to shape their contributions appropriately and ensure that the whole process has the proper focus which will contribute to efficiency and ensure that judgements are both appropriate and of good quality.

The emphasis now shifts from the individual workers to a consideration of their role in the system of assessment of special educational needs and the placement of pupils with such needs in suitable educational situations.

THE PROCESS OF ASSESSMENT

The Education Act of 1944, in addition to making each LEA responsible for ascertaining which children in its area required "special educational treatment", prescribed formal procedures for discovering handicapped children and placing them in schools, (Section 34). An "authorized officer" of the LEA could serve notice in writing requiring the parent of any child over 2 years of age to submit the child for examination by a medical officer in order to obtain advice as to whether the child suffered from "any disability of mind or body" and its nature and extent. A penalty (£10) was prescribed for any parent failing to present the child without reasonable excuse. The parent also had the right to request the LEA to arrange examination of a child; and parents had a right to be present at any examination, however initiated. The LEA was to consider the advice of the medical officer and reports from teachers "or other persons" and the *LEA* was to decide if the child required special educational treatment. If it were so decided the LEA had two duties: to give notice to the parent of the decision; and to provide the treatment. If either the LEA or the parents required it, a certificate was to be issued stating whether the child was suffering from a disability requiring *special educational treatment* and, if so, its nature and extent. This certificate was to be signed by a *medical officer* of the LEA. Parents had a right of appeal against the LEA decision, to the Secretary of State for Education who could arrange for another medical examiniation of the child. If he decided to cancel the certificate the LEA must cease to provide special educational treatment for the child. The certificate was also necessary if the LEA intended to refer to the Secretary of State to secure compulsory power to provide SET against the wishes of the parents.

As the system developed the use of certification was found to be generally unnecessary as LEAs sought to proceed by agreement with parents. Other prescribed documents continued to be used in the less formal process and it was still necessary for the recommendation to the LEA to be signed by a medical officer. Educational psychologists completed the psychological section of the documents, though they were not allowed to sign them, and the section could, in fact, be completed by an approved medical officer who had completed a two-week course in mental testing.

It can be seen that the medical model which resulted in the categorization of educational disabilities was also continued in the concept of *treatment* and in the allocation to medical officers of decisions about the educational needs of children as well as in the categorization of disabilities as being *of mind or body*. However, as the system was tested by time and development, and as teachers and psychologists became more experienced and more confident, the unsuitability of the system became more obvious. Criticism mounted. And it was not silenced by the informality introduced into the system. Nor was criticism entirely negative, for there was much discussion and suggestion about what should replace the current system, culminating in the design of an alternative system and the establishment of field trials by the Department of Education & Science. The outcome was DES Circular 2/75, *The Discovery of Children Requiring Special Education and the Assessment of their Needs* (Welsh Office Circular 21/75) which recommended the replacement of the process described above by one based upon a multidisciplinary approach within a firm educational framework. Such a process is now in operation.

DISTINCT PHASES IN THE ASSESSMENT PROCESS

Before describing the current system for the assessment of handicapped pupils and their educational placement, it is necessary to direct attention to differences between the pre-school years and those after the child enters the school system. The differences are considerable.

The Pre-school phase

In the meaning of the Education Act 1944 a child is any person not over statutory school leaving age, which means that the LEA has a duty to discover and assess handicapped children from birth onward. In practice this responsibility has been regarded as operating from the age of 2 years, the age at which nursery education is provided for children between that age and the age of 5 years (where facilities exist). But although the LEA has this responsibility, there is usually no direct contact between the Authority and the parents of children not in attendance at schools maintained by the LEA. It follows, therefore, that in the pre-school years the LEA depends almost entirely on outside sources for information about children who suffer from any disability. The sources of information are parents of children and health or social service workers. In this age-range it appears, then, that the LEA has responsibility but little access and no control and few Authorities would be confident that at any time they had been made aware of all pre-school children in their area who may be in need of assessment. Yet there has been growing acknowledgement of the need for early educational intervention, especially where major sensory channels are affected or children exhibit severe mental retardation; hence the development of the pre-school teaching noted above.

Another point to note is that many disabilities which directly affect learning are not apparent in the pre-school years. Moderate educational subnormality is often not obvious until the child fails the first formal learning tasks in school; maladjustment in the pre-school years is rarely diagnosed; and only the most severe conditions which would cause a child to be regarded as educationally "delicate" would be so noted in infant children. Yet these categories of handicap account for more than half of the children receiving special education. In addition, these and many other disabilities may develop at later ages, even after the child is in school. Nevertheless, it is extremely important that all children with disabilities should be brought to the attention of the LEA, even if the effect of the disability on learning is not assessable. The LEA will be forewarned and assisted in its planning, while it may be possible to arrange intervention which will eliminate or reduce the effect on learning of some disabilities.

An organization which will develop in the future is the District Handicapped Team as proposed in the Court Report, *Fit For the Future* (1976)[1]. The DHT will be a Health Service responsibility but the cooperation of the LEA will be necessary if it is to function properly in relation to children. It is not always realized that the function of the DHT will be mainly in the pre-school years, limited mainly to seriously disabled children, and that it will not replace the current procedures (or whatever replaces them) for the majority of children with special needs. But this is clear from four points in the Court Report.

1.   The report agrees that many handicapped children will first be noticed in schools by their teachers who should be free to use their own judgement and seek the advice of colleagues (14.21).
2.   Only a minority of children will have severe disorders, difficult to diagnose and requiring intensive investigation. Most disabilities will be only moderate, and intensive comprehensive assessment for them is neither warranted nor possible (14.17).
3.   For most handicapped children the report agrees that the procedures set out in DES Circular 2/75 are appropriate, and it commends the practical advice on assessment in the circular (14.21).

4.   The report considers that it would be a mistake to separate the special health services for handicapped children from those which all children receive in school, so the primary health care team should provide the main Health Service contribution in quantitative terms to the diagnosis, assessment and treatment of handicapped children (14.19).

The School Years

The law relating to school attendance and the arrangements made by LEAs to ensure that parents comply with the law ensure that from the age of 5 most pupils are on a school register except those unfit to attend school or being educated under arrangements made by the parents which are acceptable to the LEA. The responsibility of the LEA to discover and assess children in need of special education has not changed, but now the LEA has access and control over the situation. Furthermore, children are beginning to be exposed to the formal learning tasks involved in education, and observation in this situation provides high-quality information for use in the process of assessment. The medical services to the schools are now more intimately related to the education service; the school welfare service relates the schools directly to the child's home and parents; and if social services are involved with the family the probability of contact with the school is greatly increased. As a result the certainty of discovery is markedly improved and the situation is conducive to improvement in the quality of assessment. The situation is also improved by the fact that the new system of assessment (described on pages 32-7) fits the school situation more easily than that of pre-school assessment. Against this, the "distancing" of parents from the schools which occurs from infant school onwards creates a special problem in later assessments and a positive effort is required to ensure that the views of parents are adequately represented. Nor would it be correct to assume that the assessment system works perfectly once under the control of the LEA. Milder losses of sight and hearing still too often exist undiscovered in the schools. Pupils are too often put up for assessment long after the point at which their needs should have been obvious to their teachers; once brought to notice a child's assessment may be slow in starting or unduly prolonged in execution; and the quality of educational, social, medical or psychological information may leave something to be desired. In some LEAs good quality assessment may be frustrated because the Authority has failed to match it with a sufficiently wide variety of educational provision or through a shortfall in the amount of provision. Also, there is still a problem in securing full integration of the medical input to assessment now that the school medical service is outside educational control; and a lesser, though none the less real, difficulty in securing full integration of social services input. These problems are often operating in cases where assessment is unduly delayed or extended.

It would be unwise to assume from the above criticisms that the discovery and assessment of handicapped children is in a state of chaos, though this is implied in some of the views expressed by those who see only the cases of failure rather than the operation of the system as a whole. A survey of 1,500 consecutive assessments in a large LEA recently showed that two out of every three assessments were completed from start to school placement in a period of two to four months. Only one case in six extended beyond four months and in many of these the delaying factor was that the parents responsible for the child failed to keep appointments or they were temporarily outside area of the LEA. But this is no reason for complacency. However few the delays, the fact is that they may be critical for the children concerned, and this weighs heavily on anyone responsible for operating the system. No effort is too great if it eradicates delays or inadequacies in meeting the needs of handicapped children.

THE NEW SYSTEM OF ASSESSMENT

The principle of the new approach rests in a more positive attempt to regularize the contribution of the different disciplines to the assessment process and to place them in an appropriate educational frame of reference. The former emphasis on the medical officer as the person to offer advice to the LEA has ended. That role is now the responsibility either of educational psychologists or inspectors/advisers in special education. It is, however, necessary to secure the cooperation of parents and teachers as well as doctors and social workers and to consider their advice before a recommendation is made to the LEA. The documents designed for use in the new system have the objective of securing interdisciplinary information about the pupil's disability. There are no special forms for the collection of inputs from parents or social workers and many LEAs have designed local forms for that purpose. The system is intended to operate as follows.

Initial Discussion

Circular 2/75 makes clear the fact that the system of assessment begins when a pupil first reveals difficulties in school. At that point there should be discussion in the school in an attempt to find a solution to the problem presented by the pupil. It is appropriate that the parents should be informed at this point as they may have information that will be helpful to the teacher and may be alerted to the child's needs. Where necessary educational advisers or educational psychologists should be consulted, but only where the teachers are of the opinion that they require assistance or advice from outside the school. For many pupils problems will be resolved at this level while for others there will be a consensus that satisfactory progress is being made by the pupil.

There will, however, be pupils for whom it is clear that there should be more rigorous investigation of their needs or where there is good reason to believe that special education is required. This point should always be specifically discussed with the school educational psychologist or a special education adviser before the next procedure is started.

School Report

Once there is agreement that there should be full assessment of the pupil's special educational needs the headteacher of the school arranges the completion of a full educational report. This is compiled on a form designated as Form SE1. It is appropriate also that at this point the educational welfare officer (EWO) for the school should begin to assemble a social report for which most of the information will exist if the initial discussion has been properly organized. No special form exists for this report unless one has been designed in the LEA. Form SE1 sets out the pupil's educational status in terms of his attainments, learning difficulties, attitude to learning, to teachers and to other pupils, describes the pupil's behaviour in class and around the school and allows for a summary of the child's needs by the teachers and their suggestions about what is required to meet them. Where appropriate, examples of the pupil's school work may be attached to Form SE1. It is important to note that the form is not intended to be a replica of the school records but a means of bringing together all the educational information about the pupil which is relevant to the assessment of special educational needs and, where necessary, decisions about the form of special education that will effectively meet them.

The transmission and handling of the form will vary in different LEAs, but however that is arranged it should be brought together with the social report and forwarded to the next stage.

Medical Report

By whatever administrative arrangements operate locally the school and social reports will be received by the school medical officer who will already have been alerted through the initial discussion and should have much of the medical information required in his records of the pupil. He may, however, wish to examine the pupil and have the opportunity of a further discussion with the parents before completing Form SE2 which is designed for the medical report. It is important that it is realized that the form is not intended to be a complete medical history of the child in education; that remains in the school medical record which is the property of the Health Service. Form SE2 should be completed by the doctor to include all those aspects of the pupil's medical status relevant to the assessment of his special educational needs. For this purpose the doctor completing the form will make use of any specialist reports in the record, but the reports themselves will not form part of SE2. There will be cases where the medical officer completing Form SE2 may wish to consult colleagues about the pupil or even refer the child for their examination before completing the report. Efficient initial discussion could allow such arrangement to be made in advance thus saving time, and it is helpful, where the arrangements involve delay, if there is a proce-dure through which the LEA may be advised of the possible delay. Form SE2 is a comprehensive document which must allow for the full range of disabilities likely to face a doctor over a period of time. It has many sections and is divided into items which allow completion by a series of ticks with detailed information written in where necessary. Consequently, for example with moderate ESN children, their status may be perfectly normal in many sections with nothing to note. It is helpful if the doctor indicates in some way that these sections do not apply or the pupil is normal, rather than just ignoring them and leaving them blank. On completion Form SE2, together with school and social reports, is returned to the LEA.

Psychological Report

The educational psychologist will receive the completed school report, social report and medical report and she will wish to conduct a psychological examination of the pupil unless she has recently completed one. The results of her examination are entered on Form SE3. Sections of the form cover intellectual status (including results of intelligence tests); descriptions of pupil behaviours (with results of any relevant tests used); information about family relationships; accounts of pupil interests and attitudes as expressed or revealed during the examination; and, where appropriate, indication of the pupil's social competence and adjustment as assessed or revealed by tests. The layout of the form is similar to that described for the medical report and the psychologist also may write in information, summarize her views and indicate her recommendation about the type of placement most likely to meet the pupil's special educational needs. She may, of course, reach a conclusion that the child's needs could be met in the normal school situation, in which case she may indicate the measures that the school might adopt to ensure progress for the child. In some cases psychologists find it advisable to attach more complete reports of testing, or more detailed expression of their findings in papers attached to Form SE3.

Before describing the final part of the assessment process it is necessary to add some comment on the process so far described. At each point in the assessment the parent is entitled to be present with the child and most professional workers would have it so. This means that parents may have expressed their views to teachers, doctors, social workers or EWOs and to the psychologist. Each of these workers is free to include in his report an account of the parents' views and this is frequently part of the reports. So though there is no direct form for a parental contribution this does not mean that their views are not reflected in the assessment information. Nevertheless, they are not *directly* expressed in writing by the parents. Another comment applies to the assessment of pupils who are possibly maladjusted where there is psychiatric involvement through a child guidance team. The medical report form (SE2) does not allow for adequate expression of psychiatric reports and these need to be presented as attached reports. Some LEAs, in cooperation with psychiatrists, have produced local forms which allow for full expression of the views of the child guidance team. Where these are used it is common practice for the school medical officer to complete the general medical report (SE2).

Recommendation to the LEA

When the above examiniations have been completed and the reports are assembled through arrangements made locally, it is necessary for them to be reviewed and considered before a recommendation is made to the LEA setting out the special educational needs of the child and the most appropriate arrangements for meeting them. This will only be necessary where the child has needs which cannot be met in the normal school situation. The responsibility for this task may fall to an educational psychologist or an inspector/adviser in special education *who has seen the child under consideration*. The professional making the recommendation may find it necessary to consult colleagues about aspects of their reports, or may even feel that a face-to-face conference of all concerned is necessary before reaching a decision. In some cases a further meeting with the parents may be necessary. Finally a recommendation will be made to the LEA by completing Form SE4. This form has the general layout of the series, each section corresponding to a summary of school, medical and psychological reports and completed by ticks in appropriate places with information written in as necessary. The final section allows the person completing the form to indicate broad special educational needs and to indicate the type of special education placement which it is considered would meet the indicated needs. It is also a requirement that the form should indicate the point at which the child's needs and placement should first be reviewed. The information in Form SE4 is sufficient for a "first sort" of possible educational placements for the child and is an adequate document for monitoring reviews, but access to the full range of SE forms is necessary for the schools or other situations in which the child may be placed and for the teachers who must teach him. However, each form indicates that it is for use by professional persons concerned with the child and it is not usually considered that parents should have access to the forms.

Once the recommendation in Form SE4 is accepted by the LEA the duties of the Authority remain as in the earlier system: the parents must be informed of the decision and of their right to object; and the Authority must provide the kind of special education that has been recommended. These duties form part of the responsibilities of the AEO/SE. There is a statutory notice for informing the parents but is is usual for an officer of the LEA to visit them with a letter which explains the situation in non-legal terms and takes account of the natural anxiety which parents may feel. However, where the spirit of Circular 2/75 has been effective and parents have been closely involved in the assessment process, they will already have a good understanding of the situation and the letters and visits may be less formal and more supportive. Where there is parental disagreement with the recommendation and this is not resolved in consultation with officers of the Authority, it may in rare cases be necessary to use legal procedures. These remain at present as described for the earlier system until existing legislation can be changed. Parental rights and LEA duties relating to them also remain unchanged.

It will be seen that the system of assessment is most closely related to situations where the child's special educational needs are revealed in school. Nevertheless it does, with modification, meet the needs of pre-school children. For these the process is usually initiated from medical sources or by parents and the educational aspect comes later. Except where pre-school peripatetic teachers are involved, the educational aspect may be marginal, or theoretical, in that the teacher allocated to participate may be experienced with the age range and the disability but not with the particular child being assessed. Educational inputs of this kind may require modification of Form SE1 and cannot carry the weight of inputs based on intimate knowledge of and experience with the child. They are best regarded as general indicators of possible educational need and have an importance in making parents aware of educational considerations at an early stage in their child's development.

One other SE form remains (SE5) and this is for use when the parent is a member of the armed forces.

SUMMARY

In this chapter the people engaged in the process of assessment have been indicated as parents, hospital staff, health visitors, social workers, voluntary societies, educational welfare officers, peripatetic pre-school teachers, educational psychologists, inspectors/ advisers in special education, assistant education officers for special education (AEO/SE), medical officers, medical consultants, and teachers. Psychiatrists, psychologists, social workers and psychotherapists who form the teams in child guidance clinics are also involved with children with emotional or behaviour disorders, most of whom will be clients at the clinic. Not all workers will be involved with every child, the combination and weight of contribution depending upon the child's circumstances and needs.

The early approach to the assessment of handicapped children was consistent with a medical model, related to categorization of need and the concept of *special educational treatment*. Important differences between pre-school and school-age assessments were indicated, the LEA having responsibility but little access and no control in the pre-school phase. A recent development in the assessment process has removed the responsibility for advising the LEA on a child's educational needs from the medical officer and placed it on the educational psychologist or inspector/ adviser in special education. The system is interdisciplinary involving educational, social, medical and psychological reports using specially-designed forms. The system is seen as more suitable for use in the school system than in pre-school years though, with modificiation, it meets assessment needs at that level.

NOTES AND REFERENCES

1 DHSS (1976) *Fit for the Future*, Report of the Committee on Child Health Services, HMSO.

3

EDUCATION FOR CHILDREN
WITH SPECIAL NEEDS

LEGISLATION

Until the passing of the Education Act 1944, the education of handicapped children was governed by the Education Act 1921. Part V of the Act dealt with "Blind, Deaf, Defective and Epileptic children", the term defective relating to physical and mental disabilities. This part of the Act was separated from those dealing with elementary schools and with higher education so that though LEAs had a duty to provide education for blind, deaf, physically defective, epileptic and mentally defective children, that duty was seen as separate from the general education provided at elementary and higher level. For blind and deaf children education was to be given in a school "certified by the Board of Education as suitable" and similar certification was required for any school or class set up to provide education for epileptic or defective children. The Act also defined the categories of handicapped children, for example the defective:

> . . . not being imbecile, and not being merely dull or backward, are defective, that is to say, . . . by reason of mental or physical defect are incapable of receiving proper benefit from instruction in the ordinary public elementary schools, but are not incapable by reason of that defect of receiving benefit from instruction in such special classes or schools as under this Part of this Act may be provided for defective children [55. 1(a)].

Provision of special schools varied greatly throughout the country, being concentrated in the large towns and cities but nowhere adequate. As a result many pupils who would have benefited from special education were left in ordinary schools. (Pritchard, 1963;[1] DES, 1978[2]).

The Education Act 1944 changed the above situation. Each LEA now had a duty to provide for all children within its area education according to "age, aptitude and ability" and this included what the Act termed *special educational treatment*. Plans to provide SET were to be included within the general planning of primary and secondary education while, in addition to special schools and classes, arrangements could be made to educate less seriously handicapped pupils in the ordinary classes of primary and secondary schools. As the education of handicapped children in these classes is frequently regarded as a recent idea, it is interesting to examine the words of the 1944 Act in detail. Local education authorities were to have regard to:

> the need for securing that provision is made for pupils who suffer from any disability of mind or body by providing, either in special schools *or otherwise*, special educational treatment, that is to say, education by special methods appropriate for persons suffering from that disability [Section 8.2(c)].

Or, to quote Section 33.2:

> The arrangements made by a local education authority for the special education of pupils . . . shall, so far as is practicable, provide for the education of pupils in whose case the disability is serious in special schools appropriate to that category, but where that is impracticable, or where the disability is not serious, the arrangements may provide for the giving of such education in *any school* maintained by a local education authority or in any school not so maintained other than one notified by the Secretary of State to the local authority to be, in his opinion, unsuitable for the purpose.

Section 33.1 made it the duty of the Secretary of State to define the categories of handicapped pupils and to make provision as to the special methods appropriate to each category. Categories were defined through the issue of a Statutory Instrument (see Appendix 1) which also set down the conditions necessary for the recognition of a special school; so far as special methods were concerned, only the maximum number of pupils to be allowed in any class appeared relevant, and the number was defined for each of the categories. Otherwise education was to be suited to the age, ability and aptitude of the pupils with particular regard to their disability of mind or body, they were to attend religious worship and have religious instruction in accordance with the wishes of parents, with neither to apply contrary to parental wishes.

Since the Act was passed, other official sources have confirmed the desirability of providing special education in ordinary schools:

For the handicapped child the normal field of opportunity should be open to the fullest extent compatible with the nature and extent of his disability. The fact that he has a mental or physical handicap does not necessarily involve his withdrawal from a normal environment but, if he has to be withdrawn at all, the withdrawal should not be further or greater than his condition demands. Handicapped children have a deep longing to achieve as much independence as possible within the normal community instead of being surrounded by an atmosphere of disability, but their handicap carries with it, especially in older children, a danger of psychological and emotional disturbance, resulting from a sense of deprivation and frustration. This can often be countered by retaining them within the normal environment, or as much of it as their condition allows, provided that within it they are treated with understanding and given the fullest opportunities. (Report of the Chief Medical Officer of the Ministry of Education, 1952-3. MOE 1954.)

In *The Education of the Handicapped Pupil 1945-55* (MOE, 1956) it says:

The fact that this [special educational treatment] might be given in special schools "or otherwise" and that, in Section 33 of the Act, it was stipulated that where a child's disability was "not serious" the special educational treatment might be given in "any school"—i.e. not necessarily in a special school or even in a special class—served to emphasise that physical or mental handicap existed in all degrees, from the very slight to the serious; and that special educational treatment was not a matter of segregating the seriously handicapped from their fellows but of providing in each case the special help or modifications in regime or education suited to the needs of the individual child.

In that same publication reference is made to the Ministry of Education Circular 276 issued in June 1956 which stated as Ministry policy:

No handicapped pupil should be sent to a special school who can be satisfactorily educated in an ordinary school.

The Act also empowered LEAs to establish special schools in hospitals, or, where the number of children was below twenty-five, to arrange for special education under Section 56, "Education other than in school". The same section allowed the LEA, in "exceptional circumstances" to provide education for handicapped children in their homes.

It may be seen, therefore, that so far as the Act itself was concerned there was an expansion in the concept of special educational provision, increase in the flexibility accorded to LEAs in providing it, the introduction of the idea of range of severity in handicap, and associated stress on making provision at a level appropriate to the disability level of individual children. These were real improvements even though the deficit model of handicap, the concept of "treatment" and the categorization of handicapped pupils also operated as indicated in Chapter 1.

PROVIDING EDUCATION

The opportunities created by the 1944 Act were not realized in the provision of special education. Expansion there certainly was, as indicated by the statistics of growth in Chapter 1. But the growth was mainly in the provision of more special school places allied to expansion in the additional training of teachers working in them, with comparative neglect of provision for handicapped pupils within ordinary schools. This is reflected in the figures for 1977. Of the 156,935 pupils in special schools and classes only 21,674, or 13.8% were in the special classes (DES, 1979)[3]. A Schools Council Project which looked at the curricular needs of slow learners in 500 schools in England and Wales reported the following percentages of teachers with additional training working with slow learners: special schools 44%; secondary schools 28%; primary schools 4% (Brennan, 1979[4]). Nor should it be assumed that the expansion in special school places resolved the problems of all children recommended for places in the schools. In 1977 some 6,716 pupils of statutory school age were awaiting placement in special schools; of these, 2,293, or 34%, had been awaiting a place for more than one year (DES, 1979).

The development of special schools requires further comment. The 1944 Education Act did not lay down that special schools should be developed to accord with the categories of handicapped pupils to be defined by the Secretary of State, though Section 8 indicated that special methods were to relate to disability and Section 33 indicated that special schools appropriate to the category of handicap were required. Nevertheless that is how special schools developed. By 1977 there were 1,541 maintained special schools of which 81, or 5.3%, were classified as receiving pupils in more than one handicap e.g., delicate/physical handicap, deaf/partial sighted; only 14 schools were classified as receiving pupils who were multiply handicapped and they formed 0.9% of the special schools (DES, 1979). The LEAs alone cannot be made responsible for this situation. All proposals for new special schools require the Secretary of State's approval and inclusion in the DES building programme. It appears, therefore, that notwithstanding the brave words about provision in ordinary schools and the flexibility made possible in the 1944 Act, the central department of education did little to promote flexibility in practical terms, or, if that was done, then it was remarkably unsuccessful.

At the same time there are some logical reasons which explain the concentration on special schools. When a main system of education is under pressure there is a common tendency to isolate problems and make separate provision for them so that the main system may continue to develop more effective methods to meet majority needs. Also, the task of developing specialized sub-systems is usually easier than attempting to introduce increased variety and complexity into the main system. It is undeniable that these circumstances have operated in the development of the public system of education. In the normal course of development it might be expected that as main system problems are resolved and effectiveness improves there should be some move to incorporate the separate sub-systems within the main framework. Here, too, there is evidence in education. Periods of low pressure in the main system saw the tentative development of units for partially-hearing pupils within the ordinary schools and some growth in provision for slow learners. But the truth is that the main system has rarely been free from pressure. The reorganization of secondary education in the tripartite system; the raising of the school leaving age the move to comprehensive secondary education; the revolution in primary school methods followed by experiments in middle school organization; the extension of the new primary methods into secondary schools; the growing demand for nursery education; the exceptional growth of further and higher education; the effect of stop-go economic policies by successive governments and the continuously erosive effects of monetary inflation have kept the main system under almost continuous pressure. In these circumstances the development of the special schools sub-system may have been an appropriate and reasonably successful response. But it carries with it a serious danger: the success of the special schools sub-system may create a belief that there is no possible alternative. This ignores its circumstantial origin and endows it with an apparent inherent validity that powerfully resists challenge or change.

This discussion is not intended as a criticism of special schools. They do have serious disadvantages, though most of these arise from the separation of the pupils from their normal fellows, and for this the teachers in the schools are not responsible. The same teachers, aware of the disadvantages of the special school, have developed methods to compensate through interaction with ordinary schools and "linked" courses with colleges of further education. And they have, in many instances, developed the special methods of teaching which make it practicable to consider the education of some handicapped pupils within the ordinary schools. The main purpose of the discussion so far is to show that, though there was no legislative obstacle to the development of special education within ordinary schools, conditions may have prevented the development through facing those responsible for the system of education with an almost continuous series of problem pressures. For the purpose of a chapter concerned with the provision of education for handicapped children, and with their placement in situations appropriate to their education, the result is that available alternatives to special school placement are restricted. Furthermore, while special schools offer good opportunities for the placement of pupils with a clearly-defined major handicap, serious difficulties arise if the handicap is moderate, and needs support but not necessarily at the level of a special school. Even greater difficulty arises in placing pupils with multiple handicaps. This is not so much because special schools are unwilling to admit such pupils but because, as the schools themselves would freely admit, there is little experience in the system in meeting with an acceptable degree of success the problems these children present. The result is that anyone concerned with the educational placement of handicapped children becomes well aware of the fact that handicaps range widely from the mild to the severe and increasingly occur in multiple form for the same child. Logically it might be expected that arrangements for the education of handicapped children would follow a similar pattern. In fact they do not: and this poses a major difficulty in placement for an increasing number of children.

PLACING CHILDREN WITH SPECIAL NEEDS

Exactly which officer decides on the correct or best available placement for a child with special educational needs may vary between different LEAs. In some the educational psychologist or special education inspector/adviser who completes Form SE4 may also make the decision on placement after consulting colleagues as necessary. In others the final decision may rest with a senior psychologist or inspector/adviser. At least one large LEA has introduced a division of the task in which the educational psychologist involved completes both Form SE3 and Form SE4 but the decision on the placement of the child rests with an inspector of special education. Whichever officer makes the decision it is, in principle, a recommendation to the LEA, for it is the Local Education Authority that is legally responsible for providing special education and for placing individual children in the situation most appropriate for their special educational needs. Though much depends on the size of the LEA and upon its organization, there does seem to be an advantage in the placement decision being made by an inspector/adviser in special education. In their role they are likely to spend more time in special schools and classes than the educational psychologist who has much wider terms of reference; their experience of teaching handicapped pupils is usually more extensive; their training in and experience of curriculum, classroom organization and general school policy is wider than that of most psychologists; and inspectors/advisers, through their visits to schools outside the LEA, usually have a wider concept of all available possibilities than their psychologist colleagues. Nevertheless they will require good briefing from those colleagues where there are special considerations involving specific learning difficulties of individual pupils. It must be clearly realized that these comments refer to the role of the psychologist and inspector or adviser. An individual educational psychologist may have teaching experience far greater than the nominal two years required in the profession; and some inspectors/advisers in special education are educational psychologists.

The task of advising on the educational placement of a child with special educational needs involves bringing together two sets of information. The adviser concerned must know as much as possible about the individual child and his or her needs. This information comes from the assessment papers described in Chapter 2 including the summary in Form SE4. While these forms are an improvement on those they replaced, and though the discussion in Circular 2/75 stresses that they should describe the child's needs, the forms are, in fact, still dominated by the categories of handicapped children. The wording of items in Form SE4 and the fact that special schools are largely organized to accord with the legal categories of handicap make it very difficult to escape from the prevailing approach, though most professionals make some attempt to do so. As a result the adviser considering placement will almost certainly be considering individual schools within a category of handicap generally equating with the recommendations of Form SE4. At this point the second set of information requires consideration. Of the schools appropriate, which is most suitable for this child? To answer this question the adviser needs a great deal of information about the schools. A whole stream of questions follows. Must it be a boarding school or a day school? If a day school, which is most suitable for access in terms of travel and links with the child's family? What are the differences in the curricular strengths of the schools and which most closely matches the child's main needs? Are there any special teaching strengths in any of the schools which are particularly appropriate for this child? What are the general levels of pupil behaviour and type of discipline in the schools and how do these relate to the pupil? What is the past record of the schools in meeting the needs of children similar to this one? Have there been recent changes in any school which might affect the ability or willingness of staff to meet the needs of this child? Is any school affected by change of headteacher or staff? Will it change the evaluation of the school in any way? Have the parents expressed any preference for this or any other school? How do these schools relate to parents? Which is likely to relate best to the parents of this child? Is there one school which is clearly the most suitable for this child? Or are schools X and Y equally suitable? Should the parents be asked to visit one school and reach a decision before, if necessary, being invited to visit another? Or should they be given both schools to visit and their choice accepted? Questions like these formulate in the mind of the adviser considering the placement, and he may also labour under some frustrations: the most suitable school may not have a vacancy appropriate to the age of the child; is there a reasonable alternative or would it be better to wait for a vacancy in that school; and how long would the wait be? There may be no vacancy in a suitable school and the adviser may have to consider seeking a place outside the LEA. How would the parents view that? Would it mean boarding school? If so, is it proper to advise that the child should be educated away from home because of lack of places in the LEA? And so the questions go on.

An adviser in the above situation faces a complicated task which is made more difficult by certain features of the current situation in most LEAs. First, though the description of pupil needs is far from satisfactory, it is usually better than current techniques for describing school regimes. Second, school strengths and weaknesses usually reflect those of the teachers who form the staffs; hence staff changes often imply school changes. And though children change as they grow and develop, changes in schools are frequently much more rapid as staff arrive and leave. Third, the previous point means that a school suitable for a child when placed may lose the very strengths that had indicated the school as the most suitable choice. Fourth, however good an adviser may be, his assessment of a school has inevitable limitations. Fifth, very few LEAs have yet devised a means by which schools may keep the LEA aware of their strengths and weaknesses or the changes which affect every school. And sixth, few LEAs have a sufficient variety of special schools to allow real and meaningful choice in the placement of children with special educational needs. Furthermore, where placement with special support in an ordinary school is indicated by the child's educational needs, the choices available to the adviser making the placement are usually even more restricted than the choice of special schools. Given the situation described, it would not be an overstatement to say that ideal placements are rare and that most represent a compromise in the sense that they are the best possible and available in the current circumstances.

In view of what has been written above the efficiency of the system of special education may be questioned. Yet the fact remains that by far the great majority of placements work out well for the children and satisfy their families. How can that be? It is highly probable that the degree of success relates to the flexibility with which special schools approach the problems presented by the children placed in them. Teachers in the schools and the advisers who place children are aware that needs as at present described only very broadly indicate what the child requires. More precise definition of the pupil's needs arises during his teaching and learning in the school, and the regime is gradually accommodated to them. Add to this the natural resilience of children (often underestimated by adults) and accommodation becomes a two-way process, supported by the care and concern for children which is the outstanding feature of special schools. And these same features appear in the best work observed where children with special needs are educated within the ordinary schools. More than anything, the lower pupil-teacher ratios and the reduced pressures in special schools and classes make this possible through the intimacy which they allow between teacher and learner. But though these features contribute to success they also bring dangers. The most serious of these is the danger that the schools and classes may demand too little of the pupils in terms of their scholastic attainments. It may be that most pupils lose by this, though the main concern must be for those pupils who, though with disabilities, have the potential to follow a normal academic curriculum. In this respect those in special schools are most at risk through the small size of the schools, the limited staff numbers and the consequent restriction of the curriculum. All these considerations will be in the mind of the adviser as he contemplates the possibilities and reaches a decision about the child.

Once the decision is made the adviser will send the assessment papers with a note of his recommendation to casework sections of the LEA special education branch (sometimes known as special services) which is headed by the assistant education officer for special education. Workers in the section will arrange for parents to be notified of the school and will also inform the headteacher. Through the school welfare services arrangements are made for the pupil and parents to visit the school and have a discussion with the headteacher. If there are doubts about acceptance on either side they may be raised with the AEO/SE. A dialogue then takes place in which the situation is viewed against possible alternatives and there may be discussions between the parents, headteacher, adviser and, where thought necessary, any other professional who has been involved in the assessment of the pupil. The purpose of these discussions is to secure the best possible placement for the child, if possible through the agreement of all the parties involved. Once a decision has been made arrangements are made for the admission of the pupil to the school and his or her name is placed on the school roll.

The process has been described as it exists in many LEAs, but there are some common variations. Placement may be made through the recommendations of a placement conference where the heads of a number of schools may meet to consider the pupils thought suitable for their schools and make recommendations about which school would be best for individual pupils. It is usual for such a meeting to be chaired by the AEO/SE or an officer from SE branch and the advisers concerned with the children are also present and participate in the decision. The admissions procedure is then as described above. A similar meeting may be held, informally, by the adviser so that he has the views of head-teachers before he makes his recommendation to the LEA. Where there is difficulty in reaching agreement with parents, the same kind of meeting may be arranged with the parents present so that they may hear and evaluate for themselves the views of the different officers involved in the assessment and placement of their child. These meetings can be very time consuming and demanding, but most LEAs consider them well worth while in an attempt to secure the agreement necessary to give the child a good start in his special school.

Similar procedures to the above are necessary where a handicapped pupil is to be placed in a special class within an ordinary school, especially if it involves the transfer of the pupil from a current ordinary school. In general such a placement is more easily accepted by parents and it is not usually necessary to become involved in the long discussions that often precede placement in a special school. One complication is that in some instances (especially where difficult behaviour is involved) there may be a difference of opinion about a pupil's suitability between the headteacher of the school and the teacher with responsibility for the special classes. Yet it is important that both should be involved and, if possible, agree with the admission. Another factor is that the existence of special classes often increases parental opposition to special school placement. In these circumstances parental pressure may lead to proposals for special class placement of pupils who might be better placed in a special school, with consequent objections to admission from the head of the ordinary school on the advice of the teacher in charge of special classes.

A more common difficulty arises from a lack of special education provision in ordinary schools combined with inadequate provision of special school places. In these circumstances pupils who could profit from special education in an ordinary school cannot be so placed because the support they would need is not available in the school. Placement in a special school then becomes inevitable and is deeply resented by parents who recognize the situation. At the same time, headteachers of special schools are often reluctant to admit these pupils when they have children on their waiting lists with a much greater need for what the special school can offer. However this situation is resolved, a child is denied access to appropriate special education — at least for the time being. This represents a failure of the LEA to discover the children in its area who require special educational treatment and to make arrangements to provide it: a duty placed upon LEAs 35 years ago in the 1944 Education Act. It is not surprising, therefore, that parents, teachers and advisers become frustrated and angry about such situations.

In an attempt to do something about the above situation advisers often encourage headteachers of suitable ordinary schools to make in-school arrangements which assist children with special educational needs who require support. They may arrange for a teacher with relevant interests and skills to join the staff; or support to the school may be made available from the peripatetic service of visiting remedial teachers; and the school psychological service may allocate more psychologist time to the school. It may then become possible to place in the school some children with special needs, particularly if the need is for support in learning. It is not unknown for such arrangements to develop into a worthwhile special class but the arrangement is always at risk. If the school comes under stress of any kind the arrangement may be disbanded temporarily, to the disadvantage of the pupils; or changes in the staff of the school may cause the permanent break-up of the support. Advisers can never be totally confident that arrangements of this kind will persist for as long as they are required by the children placed in them and they cannot be regarded as an adequate substitute for purposeful planning of permanent situations by the LEA. Another possibility, especially suitable for pupils who are mildly physically handicapped or require more medical supervision than is usual in an ordinary school, is to place the pupil in a school for "delicate" children. These schools are usually larger than other special schools, the curriculum is nearer to that of ordinary schools, and the school organization is appropriate for meeting a wide range of teaching and curricular needs. Many advisers make use of these placements but few would regard them as an adequate substitute for proper support within an ordinary school.

There are times when advisers are faced with children for whom school placement is not a possibility but who none the less need appropriate education—for instance, seriously handicapped children in the pre-school years. If the LEA has organized a service of pre-school home teachers then the problem is simply one of including the child in the schedule of an appropriate teacher. In the absence of such a service (a not untypical situation) the adviser may have to consider an *ad hoc* arrangement with the staff of an appropriate special school or rely on the fortuitous availability of a teacher willing to visit. Exactly the same situation exists where children are unable to attend school and must be educated at home—whatever their age. A child in hospital where there is no hospital school presents the adviser with similar problems. Either a hospital school must send in a visiting teacher or a part-time teacher must be found for the task, which is complicated by the need to relate teaching to the curriculum of the school to which the child will return.

It has become apparent in the discussion that advisers responsible for the school placement of handicapped children in situations where facilities are inadequate or restricted face a daunting task. In smaller LEAs it is not unusual for the special education adviser/inspector to have a whole range of other duties in ordinary schools. These include: organization of in-service training; advice to schools on internal arrangements to meet the needs of slow learners or other pupils with problems; advice on suitable books and equipment for the task, and guidance on the appointment of teachers for work in these schools. At the same time, the AEO/SE will, no doubt, be looking for advice on how to improve the inadequate service. Though the educational psychologist can share some of this task, he cannot share the professional supervision of the schools or responsibility for the quality of special education. An adviser may be in discussions with parents who are unaware of his workload and regard him as being exclusively concerned with the education and well-being of their handicapped child. Considerations of this kind have resulted in proposals by the Warnock Committee for improved advisory services and these are discussed in Chapter 4.

THE RANGE OF SPECIAL PROVISION REQUIRED

Provision in different LEAs varies so much that to select and describe a typical situation would be misleading. It is proposed, therefore, to list the reasonable range of provision which should enable an education authority to meet most of the special educational needs in its area. The list is quoted from the Warnock Report (DES, 1978):[5]

- full-time education in an ordinary class with any necessary help and support;
- education in an ordinary class with periods of withdrawal to a special class or unit or other supporting base;
- education in a special class or unit with periods of attendance at an ordinary class and full involvement in the general community life and extra-curricular activities of the ordinary school;
- full-time education in a special class or unit with social contact with the main school;
- education in a special school, day or residential, with some shared lessons with a neighbouring ordinary school;
- full-time education in a day special school with social contact with an ordinary school;
- full-time education in a residential special school with social contact with an ordinary school;
- short-term education in hospitals or other establishments;
- long-term education in hospitals or other establishments;
- home tuition.

The list is not exhaustive. Nevertheless, consideration of it in relation to the placement difficulties outlined in this chapter shows that the range of provision, with sufficient places, would resolve most of the difficulties. It is interesting, too, to compare this list with the description of a LEA provision on page 15.

Another effect of the range of provision would be to create pressure for more careful and detailed descriptions of children's special educational needs so that placement among the wider possibilities may be made more accurate and appropriate. Similarly, the same pressure would operate to make reassessment more sensitive in order to utilize the range of provision available.

SUMMARY

This chapter has shown how the Education Act of 1944 placed special education firmly within the frame of ordinary education, made possible provision in ordinary schools, widened the scope of special educational treatment and extended the definitions of handicapped pupils. But it also showed that the opportunity to provide special education in ordinary schools was neglected and expansion confined mainly to special schools. The lack of ordinary school provision penalized most those pupils who could have followed a normal school curriculum with support. Multiply handicapped children were also difficult to place in schools developed to reflect specific categories of handicap.

The process of placing handicapped children in special education has been described and shown to be complex, in particular because of the lack of ordinary school provision allied to a general shortage of special school places. Methods used by advisers to overcome this are indicated but found to be at risk of disbandment when schools are under pressure to the disadvantage of the pupils. The range of questions which arise in placing children has been illustrated and the difficulty of matching needs and facilities brought out. It is considered that the success which exists is because the descriptions of needs are but broad indicators which are refined in the schools as they adjust to pupils and pupils to the schools.

The range of provision required if LEAs are to carry out their responsibilities is illustrated. It is suggested that the range would resolve most problems and lead to improvement in assessment, placement and review procedures.

NOTES AND REFERENCES

1. PRITCHARD, D.G. (1963), *Education and the Handicapped*, Routledge and Kegan Paul.

2. DEPARTMENT OF EDUCATION AND SCIENCE (1978), *Special Educational Needs*, HMSO.

3. DEPARTMENT OF EDUCATION AND SCIENCE (1979), *Statistics of Education Vol. 1, 1977*, HMSO.

4. BRENNAN, W.K. (1979), *The Curricular Needs of Slow Learners*, Evans Methuen Educational.

5. DES (1978) *op. cit.*, p.96.

4

WHAT SHOULD BE DONE?

There are four sources for the material in this chapter. The first is the continuing debate about special education among parents, educationists and the general public which has been reflected in the comments of previous chapters. That debate led to the second source, the *Report of the Committee of Enquiry into the Education of Handicapped Children and Young People* published in 1978. Generally referred to as the "Warnock Report", it ranges widely over the subject and is the result of four years of deliberation by a large committee with representatives from education, health, social services and parent organizations. Following from the report came the White Paper *Special Needs in Education*, presented to Parliament in August 1980, which indicated the response of the government to the Warnock Report and set out a general approach to new legislation. This constitutes the third source. Then in the spring and summer of 1981 an Education Bill passed through parliament which resulted in the Education Act 1981 (Special Educational Needs) which amended the law relating to special education and forms the fourth source for this chapter.

At this point some general indication of the content of the Education Act may be useful. In amending the law of special education it introduces the concept of special educational needs and requires each local education authority to identify and assess children in its area who may have special needs. For children whose special needs are such that the *LEA* should determine the special education provision to be made for them, the authority must make a "statement" which sets out the special educational needs of the children and the arrangements to be made for their special education. The statements must be maintained and reviewed regularly. Parents have the right of access to the statement and the right of appeal against the LEA decision. In exercising their duty to provide schools for their area, LEAs are required to have regard to the needs of children who need special educational provision and they must keep their arrangements for special education under review. This duty is shared with the governors of county and voluntary schools and the arrangements must ensure that children with special educational needs are educated with children who do not have such needs, provided that account has been taken of the parental wishes, and that the special education required can be provided in a manner compatible with the efficient education of other children and the efficient use of resources. When the LEA is of the opinion that it would be inappropriate to provide all or any part of a child's special education in a school then other appropriate arrangements may be made. Where an authority wishes to place in an independent school a child for whom it maintains a "statement" it will require the approval of the Secretary of State, and similar approval is required for the discontinuance of any special school maintained by a local education authority. The latter point extends the power of the Secretary of State in relation to special schools and the act also empowers him to make regulations setting out the conditions to be satisfied for recognition of a school as a special school. Other regulations to be made by the Secretary of State will indicate the kind of advice to be obtained in making assessments and the manner in which assessments are to be conducted. LEAs are to appoint a 'named person' for each pupil for whom a 'statement' is maintained. The named person will assist parents in their relationship with the LEA and generally seek to further the welfare and education of the pupil. Teachers are also to be appointed for work with young persons entering Senior Training Centres conducted by social service departments.

The main criticism of the government approach has centred on the fact that the proposals are narrow and restricted in comparison with the general debate and the report of the Warnock Committee. It appears that this results from a determination that there should be no increase in expenditure on special education, a point made in both the White Paper and the Explanatory and Financial Memorandum to the Education Bill, though the White Paper did indicate that the expenditure on special education would be maintained against inflation at least until 1983-4. The White Paper also indicated that many of the Warnock recommendations did not require government legislation or comment and "do not entail significant additional resources". While this may be true of parts of the report, there is no way in which the major recommendations for increased pre- and post-school special education and its extension in ordinary schools can be implemented without increased resources. It is against this background that the rest of the chapter discusses what *should* be done.

A BROADER CONCEPT OF SPECIAL EDUCATION

The broader concept of special education is in direct contrast to the categories of handicapped children which operated before the Education Act of 1981. For the categories that Act substitutes the concept of *special educational needs* taken directly from the Warnock Report. A description of the special educational needs of the individual child becomes the objective of the assessment process; while special education consists of the arrangements made to meet the described needs—wherever those arrangements may operate. In the report, special educational needs were seen as those which required special provision in the location, content, pace, timing or methods of education; broadly, physical, sensory or mental disabilities and emotional or behavioural disorder but including any other condition, or combination of conditions, which create educational difficulties for a child which cannot be resolved by a teacher, unaided, in the classroom. Special educational needs require:

> the provision of special means of access to the curriculum through special equipment, facilities or resources, modification of the physical environment or specialist teaching techniques;
> the provision of special or modified curriculum;
> particular attention to the social structure and emotional climate in which education takes place. (DES, 1978.[1])

While special education is to be identified by:

> effective access on a full or part-time basis to teachers with appropriate qualifications or substantial experience or both;
> effective access on a full or part-time basis to other professionals with appropriate training; and
> an educational and physical environment with necessary aids, equipment and resources appropriate to the child's needs. (DES, 1978.[2])

The Warnock Committee saw this approach as one which would bring many more children within the scope of special education and for two main reasons. First, the concept of special educational needs extends beyond consideration of specific disability and takes account of the total situation of the pupils as it affects their education. Second, in addition to pupils with permanent special educational needs, there are others who will have special needs at some point in their educational development, though the needs will not be permanent. At any one time, one in six children are likely to require special education while one in five will require it at some point during their school career. These, of course, are the planning estimates made by the Warnock Committee and experience suggests that there will be wide variation between different, individual schools.

At this point it should be noted that the 1981 Education Act lacks the precision of the Warnock Report. In the Act children have special educational need if they have learning difficulties which call for special educational provision to be made for them; learning difficulty being defined as having significantly greater difficulty in learning than the majority of children of their age, or a disability which prevents or hinders them from making use of educational facilities of a kind generally provided in the schools of their education authority for children of their age. In turn special educational provision means, according to the Act, educational provision for a child over the age of 2 years which is additional to, or otherwise different from, the educational provision made generally for children of that age in the local education authority. If the child is under the age of 2 years any kind of educational provision is to be regarded as special education. In contrast with these rather vague definitions is the specific enactment that a child is not to be taken as having a learning difficulty solely because the language—or the form of language—in which he or she may be taught is different from that which has at any time been spoken in the home. These definitions leave open the question of the point at which a learning difficulty is to be regarded as significant. But, more important, they refer assessment to local conditions and do nothing to promote the kind of national standard required if equality of educational opportunity is to become more than an empty phrase.

The broad concept of special education should not be taken to imply that one child in five with special educational needs will be handicapped in the sense of the categories of handicap created as a result of the 1944 Education Act. Part of the broader concept is the recognition that there are many real needs in young children which affect their learning—often in a temporary manner- generate frustration from failure, reduce the benefit which should accrue from education and build up to serious obstacles to learning. Early recognition of the needs followed by appropriate action intervenes in the above cycle, rescues the child from the negative situation, and for many prevents the development of more serious problems. This should form much of the special education provided in ordinary schools and it will also form the major part of the extension of special education implied in the broader approach of the Warnock Report. It is to be regretted, therefore, that the Education Act 1981 places its main emphasis on provision for children whose special education is the subject of a statement by the LEA and consequently does not stress the importance of preventative special education within the ordinary school and the needs of the large number of children who require special provision though not at the level which merits a statement by the Authority. In a similar manner, the Act empowers the Secretary of State to make regulations governing the recognition of a school as a special school but does nothing to establish the basic facilities to be made available in ordinary schools which provide education for children who are the subject of a statement of special educational needs. These omissions in the Act will not prevent any LEA from making excellent special educational provision in its ordinary schools but they could lead to ill-conceived attempts at "integration on the cheap" as an alternative to special schools in a period of financial stringency.

On one thing the report and the Act agree: special schools will continue to be required for some children with special educational needs. Children in special schools will, initially, be regarded as having special educational needs determined through a statement by the LEA, though, in due course, the individual pupils will be reassessed. As valid and appropriate designated provision is made in ordinary schools for the special education of children with needs determined by the LEA the effect will be felt in the special schools in a manner to be discussed in Chapter 5, but it is too early to assess either the speed or extent with which the development may take place in the absence of adequate resources.

However, the long-term consequences of the operation of the broader concept of special education can be anticipated. Gradually there should be considerable extension of special education provision within the ordinary schools, mainly consisting of pupils whose needs were not previously recognized in any organized manner, but including also some children who might formerly have been placed in special schools. At the same time the recognition that special educational need may be temporary, or may change as the child develops, requires improvement in the flexibility with which the system of special education responds to changing needs in children and young people. This will not be achieved unless there is considerable interaction between the different situations in which special education is offered: that is, between teaching in ordinary classes, in special classes organized within ordinary schools and the designated classes in those schools which are initiated by the LEA, in support groups within the school or on other premises and in the special schools. Full use of the flexible system will require improved methods for assessing and describing special educational needs and the school regimes necessary to meet them, allied to more sensitive and regular reviews of children's needs. At this point it may be useful to give further consideration to what is implied by the Warnock concept of special educational need.

In recommending the abandonment of the existing categories of handicap and their replacement by the description of the special educational needs of individual children, the Warnock Report recognized that there would still be a need for descriptive terms for groups of children with similar special needs. The existing descriptions of children with sensory or physical disability (blind, partially sighted, deaf, partially hearing, physically handicapped) are considered acceptable. The term "maladjusted" is considered serviceable so long as it is understood to imply ". . . that behaviour can sometimes be meaningfully considered only in relationship to the circumstances in which it occurs", in which form it is considered that advantages outweigh disadvantages. But the committee regarded the term "educationally subnormal" as imprecise, assuming agreement on what was educationally normal, and suggesting intrinsic deficiency for what are mainly social and cultural deficiencies. The term "educationally subnormal" should be abandoned and replaced by the description "children with learning difficulties". To accommodate the wide range of learning difficulties a level should be indicated: "mild" to describe pupils whose needs might be met within the resources of an ordinary school; "moderate" for those pupils with needs that require placement in a special school or a designated class in an ordinary school; and "severe" for the mentally handicapped children currently designated as ESN (severe).

Presumably the current category of "delicate children" will also disappear. Those children with illnesses which generate physical disability or require special medical attention may join the physical disability provision, or, where the effect is mainly on learning, the learning difficulties group, the precise placement being indicated through the description of their special educational needs. Similarly, where illness affects behaviour, the needs of many children may best be described by the new meaning of

maladjustment. It is important to note, however, that the terms
are merely descriptions of children with similar needs: they are
not categories of handicapped children, and they have no legal
meaning in terms of the 1981 Education Act. The decision about
special education is to rest on the needs described for the child
and the measures proposed to meet them and *not* upon whether
or not he or she can be placed in a legally-defined category of
handicap.

PLANNING THE DEVELOPMENT

The changes implied in the Warnock Report will require more
than the broadening of the concept of special education. To
achieve that objective requires the extension of special education
into the pre-school years and its continuance into further and
higher education, improved contributions from the supportive
health and social services, and a degree of cooperation between
the three services only rarely achieved at the present time. All
these things make demands on expenditure. More buildings,
improved equipment, additional professional and other workers,
improved standards of training, and better information services
for parents and the community will increase demands on central
and local government budgets at a time when central government
is unwilling to increase expenditure and is also applying maximum
pressure on local government in an attempt to reduce their expenditure. In these circumstances bringing about the changes will not
be an easy or a short-term task. The circumstances call for careful
and efficient planning of the transition to the new system, for
cooperative approaches by the three services to make maximum
use of scarce resources as well as the integration of voluntary
effort in public planning to avoid unnecessary duplication of
effort and to ensure that initiative or enterprise is fully utilized
wherever its origin may be.

But even if the economic situation were easier, the transition
would still require efficient and cooperative planning and it would
be neither wise nor expedient to move rapidly across the whole
front of special education. Some of the necessary changes have in
them an inescapable time element. Education, health and social services must abandon their suspicion of each other; improved teacher
training cannot be achieved overnight; and public attitudes to the
disabled will take time to become more accepting and less patron-
izing. Within the schools themselves attitude changes are necessary
if change is to be effective. Teachers in the ordinary schools need

time in order to become confident that they can educate children with special needs in their schools and to realize that doing this for some children is not a "second best" or cheaper alternative to a special school. Teachers in special schools also need time to realize these same things and to admit that some of their children might, in fact, receive a more appropriate special education in an ordinary school. Both need to lose their sense of exclusiveness as a necessary condition for easier and continuous interaction between ordinary and special schools for the benefit of children with special needs.

Changes in teacher education are crucial. All teachers in initial training need to be made aware of special educational needs as something they will meet in schools, should be able to recognize in a general manner in the early stages and allow for in their work. They should be aware of a teacher's potential contribution to the assessment of the pupil's needs and to meeting them where it is possible in the ordinary classroom. This should be backed-up by a general awareness of the sources of support for classroom teachers in their work with children with special needs, and for the children directly, which is related to some knowledge of the different forms of special education. During their training the young teachers should have some contact with special schools and classes. That element of training is present in some courses; it requires urgent extension to all. LEAs can do little about the development except exert pressure on those who prepare teachers. But they do have control over the in-service education of the teachers in their schools. The Warnock Committee estimated that about three-quarters of the existing teaching force required additional courses to establish the objectives proposed for initial training. Clearly this is a task for LEA action and most now have a cadre of experienced teachers and advisers who could conduct the courses, if necessary with cooperation between adjacent LEAs. An important part of this work will be to make teachers aware of local support services and skilled in their use, while induction courses to achieve it will be necessary for experienced teachers who join an LEA and take responsibility for children with special needs. The scope of these courses should include the introduction of teachers to the local health and personal social services. Cooperation between the services to operate joint courses would add quality to the work. Some areas are of special importance to teachers working with children with special needs. Work with parents and non-teaching assistants; peripatetic teaching and work with pre-school children; and the principles of guidance and counselling are examples which should be developed beyond the level indicated above. In addition teachers working in special education should not be allowed to lose contact with developments in teaching in major curricular areas as has sometimes happened in the past and this aspect of in-service work is important. There will be a continuing need for teachers who have studied the problems presented by children in the different groups of special educational need at the level of the current one-year full-time courses in special education. These courses may need some expansion though it should not be regardless of the quality of the courses. The provision of part-time studies at this level will probably be necessary, while if there were closer cooperation between the LEAs and institutions offering the courses, full and part-time groups could be integrated with advantage to both. At the time of writing there are clear signs that some LEAs have already started on this phase of development, others should follow and the impetus be maintained, as it will be if advisory and support services begin to operate and cooperate on district and regional levels.

The broader concept of special education will extend the area of cooperation between education, health and personal social services at local level. Special education will no longer be almost exclusively provided in special schools so some of the necessary contributions from the other partners will be required at more input points—for instance to the ordinary schools and the designated classes in them. The probability is that a greater proportion of the input will be from the local community services rather than school-based services as developed in special schools, so the pattern as well as the extent of services will change. The extension of special education to the pre-school years will create a special problem of cooperation in the intimacy of the family at this level. The post-school extension will create a different problem, for the young person concerned acquires more personal responsibility at this level, particularly in medical matters. But the responsibility is not always recognized by parents of handicapped young people, a fact which can create real problems for supporting professionals. It will be necessary to recognize much more clearly than in the past that the role of the services changes as the baby becomes a child, then a schoolchild, an adolescent and a young adult. At each stage the service to take the lead should be defined according to the needs of the client. These problems will also appear at district and regional level where the client has complex needs or resources are scarce. Thinking and planning to identify the problems and explore solutions should start at once on a cooperative basis.

A basis for cooperative planning already exists in the Joint Consultative Committees set up in the revision of the National

Health service in 1973. The committees are formed from elected members of the Area Health Authority and the Local Authority to advise the constituent authorities on matters of common concern where the interests overlap. Some strengthening of the JCCs will be necessary if special educational provision for children and young people is to be brought within their operation. One suggestion is that there should be a working party of officers concerned with children and young people with special educational needs to keep provision under continual review. Such a working party would require membership from special education, social services, health and the careers and employment services at senior officer level. This suggestion of the Warnock Committee merits examination and exploration, but there are difficulties. The working party could easily become large and unwieldy. It would have to coordinate its work with regional organizations in special education, further education and employment and the current basis for the JCC itself will require reconsideration when the Area Health Authority disappears from the Health Service administration. (DES, 1978.[3]).

Special education has a regional organization which is based on nine groupings of LEAs. At present they form a forum for discussion of common problems, discuss regional planning taking account of the voluntary bodies and undertake a limited amount of regional in-service work in special education. If there is to be more positive regional planning aimed at regional self-sufficiency their work will require strengthening. Links with the Joint Consultative Committees are desirable and the Warnock Committee suggested that the membership should be extended to representatives of health and social services, to elected members as well as officers and to teacher representatives. The planning of special education in further and higher education will require cooperation with regional and national bodies responsible for planning those areas of education. These moves, if brought about, will require extremely careful organization. Some regional conferences in special education will become exceptionally large, the administrative load from their work will correspondingly increase and their work may well change in a qualitative manner. There is a danger that the regional conferences may fall into the hands of professional administrators, or that the educational element may be swamped by the additions from other services. It will be necessary to guard against this, for to carry out its task appropriately the regional conference must remain an *educational* forum.

There are many more mundane but equally important problems to engage the attention of special educators in the LEAs.

A planning base must be established based upon some estimate of the size of special education likely to develop in ordinary schools. At its lowest level this will require space in the schools properly located in terms of the input required from health and social services. To provide space requires consideration of population trends related to a review of school buildings. And for many sensory disabilities (such as blindness and deafness) a nice balance is required between what may be provided locally on a day school or unit basis and what will be required on a residential basis involving cooperation between adjacent LEAs, or regional planning which may include the voluntary bodies. The outcome of the exercise will influence plans in many ways. The number of teachers required in special education, the levels of their training and responsibility, the number of non-teaching assistants, child-care workers and domestic staff, the workloads to be postulated to health and social services as a basis for planning their input to the schools: all these will rest on careful estimates and projections in the special educational section of the LEA. They will be the direct responsibility of the assistant education officer for special education and he in turn will rely on sound educational advice from special education advisers or inspectors.

ADVISORY AND SUPPORT SERVICE IN SPECIAL EDUCATION

The concept of an advisory and support service (A&SS) in special education arises directly out of the recommendations of the Warnock Committee and is based upon what the members observed during their work. No doubt in the form described it is an elaboration and extension of existing good practice in a number of LEAs. In this section it is proposed first to describe such a service, and subsequently to consider why it is necessary.

First let us examine the duties of an A&SS. These may conveniently be sectionalized as work with ordinary schools, work with special schools, advice to the LEA, and advice and support for the parents of children with special educational needs.

In Ordinary Schools

The first responsibility of the A&SS in ordinary schools is to raise the quality and extend the scope of special education in them. This responsibility is shared with the headteachers of the schools and requires that the advisers work closely with the teachers in the schools. There will be a need for direct teaching of some children by the staff of the A&SS, not only to meet the needs of the child, but as an effective way of ensuring that the skills of the advisory teacher are transferred to the class teacher. To support this the A&SS has a responsibility for the organization of in-service courses for teachers in the schools and for ensuring that they have access to and make use of appropriate teaching aids and materials. Arrangements for the assessment of children with special needs must be known in the schools and headteachers will require advice on appropriate levels for individual children; they should look to the A&SS for both of these. Most important, teachers taking up work with children with special needs will need local induction courses.

In Special Schools

Here, too, the A&SS shares with headteachers the responsibility for the quality of special education in the schools. Advisory teachers will probably have less need to work directly with children in these schools though their advice will be required in relation to some children with complex or multiple disabilities, in which role they will bring to the school the specialized knowledge of members of the A&SS. A very important part of A&SS work will be to foster interaction between special schools and other situations where special education is provided; to make sure that special school teachers do not lose contact with wider developments in teaching, and to ensure that special schools do not become isolated in the system as they have tended to do in the past. There will be a need for A&SS contributions to higher level and specialized courses for teachers in special schools which will require cooperation with other A&SS and call for knowledge of the work of very specialized special schools operating on a regional basis.

In the LEA

The A&SS is the source of professional advice on the quality of special education in the LEA, assessment of its efficiency in meeting the range of needs encountered and promulgation of proposals for development. In this role the A&SS works through the assistant education officer for special education. The advisers will also be concerned about the in-school assessment of special educational needs and the provisions made to meet them, keeping the AEO/SE informed about them and making sure that the administration is aware of any inadequacies. Where children with complex or multiple needs must be placed outside the LEA advice about placement will come from the A&SS which will also be responsible for reporting on the situation and on the progress of children so placed. The LEA will also look to the A&SS for advice on the staffing of schools, the promotion of teachers, appointment of headteachers and first appointments to the Authority wherever these involve the education of children with special needs.

With Parents

The A&SS is the source of professional advice for parents about the education of their children who require special education. At pre-school level the main link will be the teachers working with children in their homes. In the school years it will mean reassuring parents about placement, school routines, outcomes of reviews or any other educational problem causing them concern which cannot be resolved by the headteacher of their child's school. There will be times when the senior adviser may become involved in complex situations where parents are at odds with the LEA. In this situation, and indeed whenever advice to parents is involved, it is important that advisers should be accorded the right to advise parents exclusively on the basis of what is best for the special education of the child, otherwise the service will be unable to obtain and hold the confidence of parents. The situation does create difficulty within an LEA, and there will be times when advisers struggle with divided loyalties, but there is a sense in which they are sometimes the defenders of the child against the LEA or even the parents. This part of the A&SS work is made more important by two interconnected circumstances: firstly, the Education Act 1981 requires LEAs to appoint a "named person" to safeguard the rights of children "recorded" as recommended in the Warnock Report. (The recorded children of the report are, in terms of the Act, children for whom the LEA maintains a statement of their special educational needs.) Second, the Act requires the LEA to *name* an officer of the authority from whom further information may be obtained when informing a parent of a proposal to assess a child's special educational needs. Together these factors may be expected to extend the responsibilities of the Advisory and Support Service in special education.

In carrying out the above important and extensive duties the A&SS will have to interact and cooperate with other sections of the LEA, for instance, the school psychological service, the school welfare service, and other parts of the local inspectorate. In addition, at the operational level, the A&SS will be the point of contact between the LEA and the health and social services in meeting the needs of handicapped children and their families.

Because of the range of local variations it is not practicable to spell out staffing levels for an A&SS, but it is possible to suggest an outline staffing structure. There is a need to have clear and unambiguous responsibility for a service as important and complicated as the A&SS so a senior adviser is required with relevant training and experience as head of the service. He will need to work closely with the AEO/SE and the head of the school psychological service but he should be directly responsible, professionally, to the principal adviser of the LEA. The main body of the service should consist of advisory teachers with a breadth and depth of knowledge about special educational needs greater than would normally be expected on the staff of a school. To them would fall the duty of continuous advice to schools about, and where appropriate the teaching of, pupils with special needs. When necessary they would call for support from the peripatetic advisory teachers described below. The work of the advisory teachers would be almost exclusively in the ordinary schools and they should be a source of expert advice on the teaching of pupils with learning difficulties and on curriculum modification necessary to meet their needs. The organization of the work of these teachers could be based upon the grouping of a number of schools or on an area of the LEA, but however determined it is important that the responsibility should be clear and adhered to. A continuous presence in their schools is an essential part of the work of advisory teachers if they are to gain the intimacy with children and staff which is essential for high-quality work. Groups of advisory teachers may be supervised by colleagues with senior responsibility for a team. Such team leaders, in addition to their general work, should have expertise in a specialized area of handicap appropriate to the level of pupils in special schools and designated classes and to them would fall the task of bringing together teachers from ordinary and special schools. They would also organize local courses. Consistent with the broad range of special education, the A&SS would need a smaller group of peripatetic specialist teachers to be concerned with children for whom the LEA has made a statement of special educational needs and who have been placed in special schools or designated classes. They will need expert knowledge of at least one of physical disability, severe sensory loss, mental disability, emotional and behaviour problems, speech or language disability and severe specific learning disability. Within the group there should be teachers experienced and trained in the special educational needs of early childhood. These are the teachers to work with pre-school children and their parents in their homes and to contribute to assessment at that level. An important part of their task will be contact with, and advice about, playgroups, nursery schools, toy libraries and other sources of educational support for the children and their parents.

All these teachers should contribute to assessment at the appropriate levels which are discussed below. But to make their work fully effective they need special links in each primary or secondary school with a teacher who has responsibility for children with special needs and is the direct link with the A&SS.

On first reading, the above organization may seem elaborate or even over-elaborate, but it is necessary. The extensions into ordinary schools make it imperative that each headteacher should have direct access to advice about children with special educational needs. The teachers responsible for teaching the children need the confidence which comes from good communication with an insightful, experienced colleague as well as the opportunity to observe him at work. And schools will require advice about their internal assessment based upon deeper knowledge and wider experience than is likely to exist on the staffs of ordinary schools. Special schools, in future, will face problems of severe and multiple handicap and more will be expected of them. The headteachers and teachers will require advice from advisers experienced in different handicaps who can contribute to the resolution of problems presented by difficult combinations of special educational need. There is also the central problem of improving assessment, in particular its educational component, and of describing school regimes so that they may be matched to the described needs of individual pupils. An informed presence in the schools is essential if these system requirements are to be satisfied. At the same time there is a pressing need to improve the quality of special education and, in particular, to promote the development of improved curriculum in all areas of special education—including the special schools. The Warnock Report contrasts the attention given to teaching methods and pastoral care with the relative unconcern about curriculum in special schools and notes the danger that the schools may be too underdemanding in what they expect of their pupils. Though exceptions were found to these generalizations in some schools visited they remain as identified system weaknesses. If there is to be progress in all these areas in the future then the development of an Advisory and Support

Service in special education, as recommended in the Warnock Report, is essential. And planning to provide it is urgent in LEAs determined to develop the broader concept of special education.

IMPROVING DISCOVERY, ASSESSMENT AND PLACEMENT

Suggestions for improving the discovery, assessment and placement of handicapped children are in no way revolutionary but reflect the best practice current among LEAs. What will accrue from the development will be an improvement in the general level of quality throughout the system of education. Nevertheless, there are some important changes of principle incorporated in the Education Act 1981. First, the concept of special educational treatment passes out of the system and is replaced by a duty on LEAs to discover all children with *special educational needs* in their area and make appropriate arrangements both for their education and for review of their progress. Second, it is clearly recognized that the LEA can only exercise that duty fully in relation to children attending LEA schools; from 2 to 5 years for children not in school and for those attending independent schools the duty of the LEA is restricted to those children brought to its attention, for instance by parents or health visitors. Third, LEAs are empowered to provide special education for children under the age of 2, though the power may be exercised only with the consent of the child's parents. Fourth, there is a clear emphasis on the need to involve parents in the assessment and placement of their children and an equally clear indication of both the right of parents to information and the extent of their access to records and reports. And fifth, the LEA has a duty to determine which children have special educational needs and these should be determined by the Authority in a statement setting out the needs and the proposals for meeting them, which must be kept under regular review.

The Act also imposes a duty on LEAs to make provision for the education in ordinary schools of children for whom the Authority maintains a statement of special educational need. There are certain conditions which must be satisfied:

1. Account must be taken of the views of the parents.
2. The child must receive the special education which is required.
3. Its provision must be compatible with the efficient education of the children with whom he or she will be educated.
4. It must be compatible with the efficient use of resources.

Within the ordinary schools a duty is laid upon the governors of county and voluntary schools. They must ensure that special education is available for pupils with special educational needs, that the special needs of children are made known to all who will teach them, and that teachers are made aware of the importance of identifying and providing for pupils with special needs. It is also the duty of those concerned with making special educational provision to ensure that, subject to the conditions noted above and where it is reasonably practicable, children with special educational needs engage in the activities of the school together with children who do not have special educational needs.

These enactments of the Education Act 1981 have been criticized by educationists, parent organizations and voluntary bodies concerned with the quality of special education. It has been held that there should be more positive legislation to establish firmly the duty of the health and social services to bring to the attention of the education service every child under 5 years of age who may have, or is at risk of developing, special educational needs. Another criticism is that the legislation concentrates on the provision of education for children who are subject of a statement by the LEA to the relative neglect of other children with special needs in the ordinary schools. Such critics point out that while the Secretary of State is to make regulations to govern the recognition of schools as special schools, he is not required to establish the basic facilities to be provided in ordinary schools, even for the education of those children in them for whom the LEA maintains a statement of special educational need. That the Act contains nothing about the need to provide trained teachers of children with special needs in ordinary schools if such placements are to be realistic, together with the position of the government in denying special education any additional resources, makes it, in the view of many critics, an educational non-event.

Discussion in Chapters 2 and 3 has already made it clear that there is a direct relationship between the assessment of pupil needs and the educational situations available to meet them. The relationship still holds in the new arrangements and until an extended variety of educational situations is made available it will be difficult to assess the degree of improvement in assessment. Much will depend upon how seriously LEAs approach the problem of development, and that may be determined by the degree of support and encouragement they receive from the DES. The discussion of the 1944 Education Act in Chapter 3 has indicated that legislation alone is unlikely to achieve any radical change in the system. Another danger arises from the fact that the Act concentrates upon changes which require parliamentary legislation. There may be nothing wrong with this from the position of central government; the danger is that some LEAs may regard what is in the Act as the total response expected from them, overlooking the many valuable recommendations of the Warnock Report which may be implemented without legislation. That said, the new arrangements are discussed in more detail.

Assessment

It would clearly be impossible to apply the interdisciplinary assessment described in Chapter 2 to the one in five pupils whose needs require assessment within the broader concept of special education. And the fact is that for most of the pupils assessment at that depth is not necessary. What is required, therefore, is a system of assessment which will meet the needs of pupils whose special education is possible within the arrangements of the ordinary school with, where necessary, advice and guidance from the supporting services. The first three stages of assessment outlined in the Warnock Report (pages 60-1) meet this need.

Stage one takes place when the pupil first exhibits difficulties in school which cannot be resolved by the teacher during the normal classroom procedures. The headteacher of the school should assemble all relevant information about the pupil's school performance together with medical, social or other information, including the views of the parents who should be alerted at this point. The headteacher and the class teacher or personal tutor then review the information and decide if any change in teaching is necessary and, if so, what changes should be introduced which are within the competence of the school. But whatever the decision, arrangements must be made to review the pupil's progress.

Stage two is similar to the above except that the headteacher decides that advice is needed from a teacher with training and experience in special education. At this point a teacher from the Advisory and Support Service will be consulted about the child and may find it necessary to carry out a personal assessment. The headteacher again consults colleagues and assembles the information. Decision will be as in stage one except that the advisory teacher may prescribe and supervise a special programme for the pupil.

Stage three may be prescribed as an outcome of the stage two assessment, or may become necessary if the pupil fails to respond to teaching arrangements established in stage two. The headteacher or school doctor, advised by the advisory teacher, may call in a peripatetic advisory teacher, educational psychologist or other supportive worker from health or social services. If the pupil's needs can be met within the school with outside support readily available then arrangements will be made as necessary. But if specialist or regular support is indicated which is external to the school then the child should be referred for interdisciplinary assessment as described below.

Stages one, two and three represent *in-school* assessment but the LEA should ensure that adequate arrangements exist for carrying out the procedures and monitoring their efficiency, particularly in reviewing pupil progress. As indicated above, this task should form an important part of the duties of the Advisory and Support Service in the ordinary schools. Some method of recording transactions at this level will be necessary if the LEA is to be kept informed of the situation and data are to be available on which to base the allocation of resources to the schools.

Criticism of the Education Act 1981 has centred on the absence of any attempt to establish procedures for the in-school assessments at stages one to three, particularly as most pupils with special needs will be assessed at these levels. The LEAs will be left to decide for themselves how they implement the Warnock Report suggestions noted above. It is still open, of course, for the Secretary of State to make regulations setting out basic procedures and minimum standards for the procedures, though it will be difficult to do this in any but the most general terms because of the variations that exist among different schools.

Stage four begins the interdisciplinary assessment established by the Education Act 1981. It is the duty of the LEA to make an assessment for any child who has special educational needs (or is thought to have them) at a level which calls for determination by the Authority. The parents of the child must be informed by a notice which gives them the following information:

1.   States the purpose of the examination, specifies the place and time and indicates the procedures to be followed.
2.   Names an officer of the LEA from whom the parents may obtain further information.
3.   Informs the parents of their right to make representations to the Authority and submit written evidence within a period stated in the notice (which must not be less than fifteen days).

Parents have the right to be present at examinations if they so desire. They also have a duty to submit the child for examination, and if they fail to do so without a reasonable excuse they commit an offence under the Act.

The Secretary of State is to make regulations about the advice which the LEA must secure in making the assessment. Educational, psychological and medical advice is mandatory, along with any other advice prescribed by regulation. Procedures to be adopted in the assessment may also be set out in the regulations together with other matters considered appropriate by the Secretary of State. But the LEA is required to consider and take account of any representations made by the parents and any written evidence which they may submit.

Clearly the assessment will require the assembly of information from teachers and social workers together with reports from medical and psychological practitioners who have examined the child, while for some children reports from speech therapists or child guidance workers will also be required. The status and qualifications of these medical, psychological and other professionals are not defined in the Act but could be the subject of subsequent regulations. However, it is in relation to parents that LEAs must act with wisdom and sensitivity. It cannot be assumed that all parents who require assistance in formulating representations or written evidence will approach the officer named as the source of further information. Many who need help may lack the initiative to seek it; others may be deterred by problems in expressing their opinions, particularly in writing. There is a moral if not a legal duty for LEAs to identify such parents, approach them with sensitivity and offer assistance in a manner calculated to secure its acceptance. Another complication arises from the assumption in the Act that assessment is a unitary process to be completed in one examination session. Only rarely are even the most straightforward assessments completed in such a manner and for some children it would be most unwise to subject them to that kind of arrangement. More typical are assessments where the different professional examinations are arranged in a phased manner considered suitable for the child and in places appropriate for the different examinations. If these cannot all be specified in the original notice to parents then a series of notices may be required. One thing is quite certain: children should not be scheduled in a manner which subordinates their needs to legal or administrative tidiness. Further, most of these problems will not arise if LEAs conduct their business in the spirit of the Warnock Report as described in the account of stage one assessment and in the discussion of the parental role in assessment in Chapter 2, for parents involved in that manner will reach stage four with an understanding of their child's needs and the confidence in the LEA which grows out of knowledge and involvement.

After consideration of the completed assessment the LEA must reach a decision about the child's special educational needs. If that decision is that it is not necessary for the Authority to determine the special educational provision to be made for the child, then the parents must be so informed in writing. Parents unable to accept the decision of the LEA have the right of appeal to the Secretary of State, who may, where he considers it necessary, direct the LEA to *reconsider* its decision. There has been criticism of this part of the Act. The rights of parents, it is contended, are not sufficiently protected and the Secretary of State should have power to direct the Authority to reverse its decision. There is some point in this criticism, though it should not be overlooked that the parents have the right to request further assessment which the LEA must grant "unless it is unreasonable". Such a request, after one or more terms with evidence that the child was not making satisfactory educational progress, could hardly be regarded as unreasonable. There is also another factor. A multidisciplinary assessment, though not resulting in a LEA statement of the child's special educational needs, should produce additional information about the child which would be of value to the teachers concerned. It is of the first importance that such information should be available to the child's ordinary school and made use of in the child's education, and the Act makes it a duty of the LEA and school governors to see that this does, in fact, occur. In any subsequent reassessment of a pupil, the use of the information by the school, together with the pupil's response, should form an important part of the available data.

Where the LEA reaches a decision that the child's special educational needs are such that the Authority should determine the special educational provision to be made, a different procedure is started. The decision must take the form of a statement of the child's special educational needs in two parts:

Part one must give details of the special educational needs revealed by the assessment.
Part two must specify the special educational provision to be made to meet the needs set out in part one.

The particular form of the statement is to be prescribed by regulation and will, no doubt, become an officially issued document.

Before the statement can become effective, the Act requires the LEA to serve a copy on the parents and inform them in writing of their right to make representations about the statement within fifteen days of receiving it. For its part the LEA is required to consider any representations made by the parents following which the Authority may:

1.　retain the statement as proposed;
2.　modify the statement in view of parental representations;
3.　decide not to make the statement.

Whatever the decision the parents must be informed of it in writing and the Authority must make arrangements for parents who wish to do so to appeal against the decision. Parental appeals go first to a local appeals committee set up under the Education Act 1980 which will see the documentation and any representations made by the parents. The committee may then:

1.　confirm the special educational provision specified in the statement; or
2.　remit the case to the LEA for *reconsideration* in view of the committee's observations.

It should be noted that in these cases the committee cannot alter the LEA decision and that it communicates with the Authority but not with the school governors. The Act requires the LEA to reconsider its decision in the light of the committee's comments following which it may retain, modify or retract the statement as noted above, notifying the parents accordingly. Parents who are still dissatisfied have the right to appeal in writing to the Secretary of State who, after consulting the LEA may:

1.　confirm the provision made in the statement;
2.　amend the statement specification of special educational provision together with any appropriate consequential amendments;
3.　direct the LEA to cease to maintain the statement.

　　The rights and duties of parent and LEA remain as outlined in any subsequent reassessment of a child's special educational needs. But the parents of a child who is the subject of a statement may themselves request a reassessment. It is the duty of the LEA to comply with such a request unless it is considered inappropriate and the reassessment must take place within twelve months. Where a child is under the age of 2 years assessment of special educational needs requires the consent of the parents. The form of assessment is to be as considered appropriate by the LEA following which the Authority may make a statement of special educational needs and maintain it as appropriate.

　　The main criticisms of the above procedures have centred upon the discretion left to the LEA in considering a parental request "unreasonable" or "inappropriate" and the vague, indeterminate nature of these terms which may lead to conflict between parents and LEAs which will be difficult to determine objectively and therefore could be a source of continuing parental dissatisfaction. On the other hand, it has been contended that the provisions for parental appeal will result in extremely protracted assessments not conducive to the task of meeting the child's special educational needs as early as possible. The resolution of both these situations rests with the spirit of the Warnock Report and the involvement of parents in the assessment process from the very start. Properly handled this may become an educational, learning experience for both sides as suggested above, resolving many misunderstandings or conflicts in the process. That this is possible is suggested by experience in one of the largest English LEAs where over five years and more than 5,000 assessments and placements, only three cases required reference to the Secretary of State for resolution.

Placement

The Education Act 1981 imposes a duty on LEAs to educate children with special educational needs in ordinary schools wherever their special education can be made available in a manner compatible with the efficient education of other children and the efficient use of resources. The headteachers and governors of ordinary schools, in cooperation with the LEA, have a clear responsibility to provide efficient special teaching for those pupils who require it and to ensure that all teachers are aware of the children with special needs. How will these enactments affect the school placements of children with special educational needs? The situation is directly affected by the decision of the government that additional resources cannot be made available for the implementation of the Act; a decision which will make it extremely difficult to provide viable special educational situations within ordinary schools. Yet until such situations are provided, the problem of placing children with special needs in ordinary schools will remain essentially as described in Chapter 3. But there is a danger. Critics of the Act have pointed out that the omission of any attempt to define the minimum facilities to be provided for children with special needs in ordinary schools may encourage improper and ineffective provision in the absence of resources. If this should occur the problems facing those responsible for placement may be increased. These points made, it now remains to examine placement in more detail.

For most children with special educational needs it will not be necessary for the LEA to make a statement determining those needs. These are the children whose special needs have been successfully assessed at stages one to three described on page 71 and their special education is the direct responsibility of the head-teachers and governors of the ordinary schools in which they will clearly remain. But the consequence of past neglect of special educational provision in ordinary schools is that, among the above group, are some children who rank as the most disadvantaged in the present educational system. If their education is to be both more appropriate and more efficient they need teachers with special training relevant to special needs who are supported by qualified and experienced advisers; they need more teachers so that they may learn in groups where they receive the individual attention which they require; they need specialized teaching materials which, at secondary level, will not be necessary for other pupils of the same age; and many require prolonged contact with individual teachers responsible for their learning, a fact which makes special demands on secondary school organization. These factors make demands on staffing and other facilities which are exceptionally difficult to provide within the present scale of resources and which cannot be provided on a wide scale without additional resources. At the same time there is contemporary evidence that resources in this area of education are being reduced. In response to central government pressure for reduced expenditure some LEAs have reduced the number of remedial teachers available in the schools, or the provision of part-time teachers whose presence often contributed to the flexibility which enabled headteachers to make arrangements for special teaching, while delays in filling staff vacancies often penalize most those children with special needs as headteachers are forced to make temporary arrangements to cover vacancies. The erosion of school allowances through failure to keep them abreast of inflation creates further difficulty as the expensive equipment necessary for some children seems exceptionally expensive in relation to the number of children who require it. Yet this negative situation should not be allowed to deter attempts to make special provision within ordinary schools. There will be isolated situations (as at present) where conditions are conducive to efficient provision. These should be exploited whenever possible in order to extend the pool of experience and to demonstrate what is possible in suitable conditions, while, utilizing this experience, LEAs should involve their schools in planning developments to be implemented as facilities become available.

Pupils assessed at stage four for whom the LEA has made a statement which determines their special educational needs will, in general, equate with pupils currently receiving "special educational treatment", most of them in special schools. Indeed, the Act empowers LEAs to regard the latter pupils as receiving special education determined by the Authority and a duty is imposed on the LEA to continue the special education provided until pupils have been reassessed and, where necessary, a statement made as required by the Education Act 1981. At the same time the Act clearly indicates that not all pupils for whom the LEA has made a statement will require education in special schools. The placement required by a pupil will be indicated in part two of the statement of his needs, and where the conditions attached to placement in an ordinary school are satisfied it will be the duty of the LEA so to place the child. Once a child with special needs is placed in an ordinary school, the Act makes it the duty of those responsible for him to secure that he interacts as far as is practicable with pupils without special needs in the activities of the school. It will be difficult for governors and headteachers to discharge the responsibilities imposed upon them by the Act in relation to pupils for whom the LEA has made a statement of special educational needs without additional resources and special support from the LEA, while the pupils themselves are unlikely to benefit from placements made in the absence of satisfactory arrangements for their special education. If, as is generally expected, the Act gradually reduces the demand for places in special schools, then it may become possible to divert some existing resources into ordinary schools. But this is unlikely to resolve the whole problem or to be sufficiently rapid to satisfy those whose objective is integration as soon as possible. There is a danger here to which critics of the Act have pointed. These pupils require teachers with special training beyond that required for teaching pupils assessed at levels 1 to 3; they have greater need for specialized equipment and health and social services support; they require an organization more distinct from that of the main school; and securing their interaction with other pupils generates special organizational pressures within the ordinary school. In these circumstances the absence in the Act of any attempt to specify the minimum facilities to be provided in ordinary schools for pupils with needs determined by the LEA may put some pupils at risk by exposing them to hasty, ill-planned attempts at integration. It is possible that this danger could be removed through regulations made by the Secretary of State but at the present time the possibility of this cannot be assessed. These considerations should not deter LEAs from the search for conditions conducive to appropriate provision within ordinary schools and where they are identified they should be exploited, for only in this manner can the possibilities within ordinary schools be demonstrated in practical terms. There should also be forward planning to create suitable conditions or to identify where they may be created as facilities and resources become available. Officer time devoted to these activities will, in the final analysis, be more productive than short-term, insufficiently-considered attempts to move pupils with statements of special educational needs into inadequate or unsuitable ordinary school situations. It is necessary to remember always that there is more satisfaction to be gained from doing things well than from merely doing them first.

Reviews

The Education Act 1981 empowers the Secretary of State to make regulations to control the review and reassessment of pupils with special educational needs. In terms of the Act this refers only to pupils for whom the LEA has made and is maintaining a statement of special educational need. If the objectives set out in the government White Paper *Special Needs in Education* are incorporated in the regulations then LEAs will be required to review each pupil annually and assess their educational progress and the suitability of their placement. The annual review need not be a full multidisciplinary review and may be conducted within the pupil's school. A full multidisciplinary reassessment would only be necessary if indicated by the school review. In addition the LEA would be required to conduct a full reassessment of each pupil's needs at least once during the primary stage of education and again during the secondary stage. Regulations such as these will face LEAs, health and social services with increased case loads and a consequent demand, in most areas, for more professionals to staff the assessment services, as it is difficult to envisage how the demand could be met within existing resources. This is not an argument against what is a necessary review system in the context of the broader concept of special educational needs, but it does highlight once more that it is extremely difficult to improve the quality of special education without the provision of additional resources.

Named Person

At the time of writing the exact point at which parents will be notified of the 'named person' is not defined. So far as education is concerned it would be appropriate to do this when parents are informed of the intention of the LEA to make a statement of special educational need. At that point parents need maximum support as they do in matters of school placement and review.

SUMMARY

In considering what should be done this chapter has introduced the Education Act 1981 (Special Educational Needs). The Act makes special educational needs dependent on a child having a learning difficulty which requires educational provision additional to, or different from, that made generally for children of the same age in the child's LEA. LEAs have a duty to discover and provide for children with such needs in their area, and, where it is considered necessary, the LEA must determine the special needs of a child through a statement which sets out the needs and the special educational provision to be made to meet them. Where the special education can be provided in an ordinary school in a manner compatible with the efficient education of other children and the efficient use of resources children with special needs must be so placed. Children with special needs who are not the subject of a statement by the LEA will receive their education in ordinary schools. Governors and headteachers of ordinary schools have a duty to provide special teaching for children who require it and must make sure that staff are aware of the children's needs.

The process for the assessment of special educational needs has been described as it takes place within a school, and the multi-disciplinary assessment required if the LEA is to determine special needs through a statement. Special importance has been attached to the involvement of parents from the beginning and through all stages of assessment and to their right of information—in particular their right to contribute to the assessment and to appeal against the decision of the LEA if they are dissatisfied. Placement of pupils with special needs has also been considered. It is contended that more alternative situations are required for the delivery of special teaching, particularly in ordinary schools, and it is held that improvement in assessment is also dependent on wider provision. At the same time it is noted that special schools will still be required for some, but not all, children with special needs determined by the LEA.

Throughout the discussion reference has been made to criticisms of the Education Act 1981. In general these have focused on inadequate consideration of the needs of children whose special educational needs are real but not at a level requiring determination by the LEA—that is, the majority of those with special needs. The absence of any attempt to establish minimum conditions for these pupils, or for those subject to statements but placed in ordinary schools, could create a danger of inadequate provision for both groups. The discussion has related these factors to the decision of the government that no additional facilities or resources should be made available for implementation of the 1981 act. The need for expanded in-service training, the essential role of an Advisory and Support Service in Special Education, the increased load on health and social services as more special education is provided in ordinary schools, and the essential need for closer cooperation between public services and voluntary organizations are described and identified as requiring more resources than are currently available. Nevertheless, it is pointed out that situations will occur where new forms of special education may be developed. These should be exploited by LEAs in order to gain experience and demonstrate their practicality and value, and there should be careful planning in anticipation of times when resources can be made available for wider development. The point at which the 'named person' should be introduced is not clear but it is suggested that an appropriate time would be when parents are informed that the LEA proposes to make a statement of special educational need.

NOTES AND REFERENCES

1 DEPARTMENT OF EDUCATION AND SCIENCE (1978), *Special Educational Needs*, HMSO, p.41.

2 DES, *op. cit.* p47.

3 DES, *op. cit.* pp 293-294, 302-304.

5

DEVELOPMENT IN THE
MEANS OF SPECIAL EDUCATION

The means of special education are those situations in which the
child or young person with special educational needs is in an
appropriate learning environment supervised by a teacher with
relevant training or experience, or both. It is here that the quality
of special education is determined. If the potential of the broader
concept of special education is to be realized then developments
in these means of education will be necessary, not only in schools
and colleges, but in other situations where teachers and learners
come together. This chapter anticipates some of the necessary
developments.

PRE-SCHOOL DEVELOPMENTS

The point has been made that the disabilities which are obvious at
birth or in the early years are those which are obtrusive or interfere
with primary functions in the young child. The need for early
intervention and family support is recognized and provided mainly
from the health and social services. The need for early educational
intervention is a more recent development, it is not widely available and is usually limited to children with major sensory loss or
severe mental handicap. This work requires development and
extension. Language disorder or delay, social deprivation and lack
of intellectual stimulation are now recognized as conditions which
generate special educational needs and can create problems in
education in later years. Similar problems arise when physical
disabilities and delayed motor activities limit experience critical
for perceptual and intellectual growth. To eliminate or reduce the

effect of these conditions a general enrichment programme is required, but it needs to be supported by the definition of critical learning objectives and the design and execution of structured activities directed at their achievement. With young children the latter activities make great demands on resources because of the need for individual teaching in a one-to-one situation, and the teacher requires training and insight in order to maintain a correct balance between enrichment and structure. The main problem is that of providing the necessary manpower for the development and extension of pre-school educational intervention.

Consideration of the above problem led to the concept of the parents as the child's first educator. Though valid for all young children, the idea is of special importance for those children at risk of educational failure, as it is just those children who have greatest need for the insights of a teacher trained in special education and experienced with pre-school children. However, if the training and experience of the teacher can be exercised through the involvement of the parents, making use of their natural intimacy with their child, then maybe the problem of manpower could be resolved. This is the starting point for the work of pre-school home teachers working within the Advisory and Support Service in special education and a first task is to extend and develop their work, placing emphasis on work with the child as an opportunity to involve the parents in the child's education and shape their contribution.

But the education of the parents extends beyond their actual work with their child. They must be made aware of and introduced to other agencies of support such as day nurseries, nursery schools or classes, playgroups, opportunity groups, toy libraries, parents' workshops and voluntary organizations. A special role for the home teacher is to inform the parents about and establish their contact with the special education situations which the child may need in later years. These wider aspects of the work cannot be carried out by the teacher unaided. At many points she will cooperate with other workers from the health and social services, and from the voluntary organizations working with handicapped children and their families. The fact is that effective intervention in the pre-school years cannot be sustained by the education service alone. The next necessary development, therefore, is an organized cooperative approach to the pre-school education of children and parents which involves the three local services and the relevant voluntary workers. Models already exist in the "Portage" project and the Hampshire replications of it, and these could be linked with Boxall's nurture group approach in the schools.

The two approaches complement each other. In Portage, project workers are trained to work with the parents of handicapped children in the pre-school years and in the child's home. Emphasis is on assisting the parent to recognize and set appropriate learning objectives for the child and to interact with the child, assisting him to achieve the objectives. Thus the parent becomes the child's first teacher, and about 60% of those involved appear to have been successful. Health visitors, social workers and pre-school teachers, as well as voluntary workers, would all have a part in this type of approach. On the other hand the nurture group, as developed in ILEA, is based in the infant school or early years of the infant and junior school. The objective is to establish a classroom regime which recaptures as far as possible the ethos of pre-school years in the home, attempting to provide the critical experiences for children deprived of them through social or cultural inadequacy or deviance. Many home-like activities feature in the work and there is special emphasis on food and cooperative dining. Combinations of these approaches could link home and school for young children with special needs; they offer opportunities for cooperation between the services and voluntary effort; and in times of financial stringency may be the means of expanding facilities within limited budgets. (DES, 1978)[1].

DEVELOPMENT IN ORDINARY SCHOOLS

The first task of development in the ordinary schools must be to ensure that children with special educational needs are discovered as early as possible so that arrangements may be made to meet their needs and increase the probability of their full participation in mainstream education; or where that is not possible, have maximum exposure to the special education which they require. The proposals for teacher training noted in Chapter 4, if effectively applied, should secure an extension of sensitive awareness of and knowledge about special educational needs in the schools. As a result, teachers should become aware of early signs of emerging difficulties and be more skilled in resolving them at a stage where they are amenable to ordinary classroom approaches. In itself this will bring about some reduction in the number of children put forward for further assessment. But if the objective is to be certainty of detection more is required. The LEAs which have established most control over the situation are those with well-established procedures for whole-year surveys of the school population on a continual, annual basis. The most critical survey is that between the ages of 7 and 8. Here pupils with mild and moderate learning difficulties begin to reveal their inadequacies in formal learning, and they form the largest group of pupils who require special education. The objective is to devise simple group tests of intellectual level and attainment and a behaviour checklist which will identify the majority of pupils with acceptable learning and behaviour. Those not cleared by the survey are then considered for assessment at the appropriate stage if they have not already been detected and assessed. Of the pupils so identified, some will have their special needs met through modifications in the ordinary schools, others will require assessment at stage four with, possibly, a statement by the LEA and placement in special schools or designated special classes. It should be noted that the Warnock Committee recommended this type of approach (DES, 1978[2]) and the development is one which does not require government legislation.

Ordinary schools have a responsibility to maintain proper records and reviews of pupils assessed at stages one to three who are not the subject of a statement by the LEA but are receiving special education in the school. Parents should be involved at each point and made fully aware of any changes in the arrangements made for their child and a common recording system in the authority would provide information valuable in planning and distributing resources. The advisory and support service should play a leading part in the development. The pupils concerned will also require appropriate special education and it will be necessary to develop options within the school to meet a range of special educational needs. Assistance within ordinary classes, withdrawal for special teaching and teaching as required in special classes are some of the options from those listed in Chapter 3, page 51. It is the responsibility of the headteacher to see that the options are established and properly used, though in many schools he will delegate this to a specially qualified member of staff who will be supported by the A&SS. Inputs from the health and social services may be required among the options. One thing is certain: special education in ordinary schools will not be a reality until the necessary options are available and are used in a flexible manner to meet special educational needs in children.

The operation of the Education Act 1981 will have the effect of making ordinary schools responsible for the education of some children with special educational needs determined through a statement by the LEA. Whatever their special needs such pupils will form three main groups. First will be those children who are capable of following the normal school curriculum if they have the non-teaching support made necessary by their disabilities. An example would be an intelligent physically handicapped pupil requiring support in order to move around the school. The second group will be formed from those pupils who require special teaching or curriculum in some areas but are able to participate in normal curriculum to a limited extent. Some pupils with physical disability, health problems or moderate learning difficulties would be in this group, with, possibly, maladjusted pupils able to participate in some normal classes if adequately supported at other times. The third group would consist of pupils who required separate teaching because of extensive sensory loss, the need for extensively modified curriculum or specialized teaching methods, or major modifications in the size or tone of the basic teaching group, but who would, nevertheless, gain substantially from social interaction in the school. The groups are not exclusive: for instance, a pupil in the second group may require the mobility assistance suggested by the example of the first group during his limited participation in normal curriculum. Examples of possible arrangements for these groups may be worked out from the list in Chapter 3, page 51 and it would be interesting to consider how the pupils described in Chapter 1 could be placed in the situations listed. Molly, for instance, is receiving full-time education in ordinary classes with periods of withdrawal to a special unit for support. John is in a similar situation except that the support he needs because of his physical condition is provided within his ordinary school. Bertie attends a day special school as a full-time pupil but has intermittent social contact with normal pupils on occasional visits to an ordinary school or with pupils from those schools who assist in Bertie's special school. At present Anne is a full-time pupil in a residential special school and her social contacts with normality are limited to out-of-school situations. Barry has most of his teaching in a special class in his ordinary school but he has full social contact within the school and limited contact with teaching in ordinary classes. The opportunities for pupils with special educational needs to interact with children without such needs should be greatly increased by the development and extension of designated special units and classes within ordinary schools.

Unlike the ordinary special classes, which may be organized by headteachers to meet the needs of pupils on the school roll who are not the subject of a statement by the LEA but require special education, designated classes or units will normally be established on the initiative of the LEA. Children may not be placed in designated classes except after interdisciplinary assessment at stage four followed by a statement of special educational needs: in other words, the pupils will have been assessed in the same manner as pupils placed in special schools. The difference will be that part two of the statement has indicated placement in a designated class or unit as being the appropriate situation to meet their special educational needs. A designated class or unit will, therefore, admit any pupil for whom it is suitable, *irrespective* of whether or not he is on the roll of the host ordinary school. The designated situation will become the base in which pupils who are the subject of a statement by the LEA receive their special teaching, special curriculum or counselling in connection with their special educational needs. But it must be more than that. The whole purpose of the situation is to create opportunity for interaction between pupils with special needs and other pupils in the school, whether in teaching, social activities or both. The degree to which this is organized for individual pupils must be determined by the pupil's needs, though the organization will require close cooperation between the teacher in charge of the designated situation, the headteacher of the school and the teachers who receive recorded pupils in their classes. Apart from consideration of the special education of the pupils, designated classes or units must conform as much as possible to the routine of the school, teachers will be full members of the school staff and teachers and pupils should participate in all appropriate extra-curricular activities. A special education adviser should have a continuing association with the special education teachers and pupils and should ensure that a balance is kept between special needs and wider school involvement. Interaction of staff, unit teachers doing some work in the school and school teachers in the unit, is a sign of a mature situation and should be fostered, while unit teachers should also maintain contact with an appropriate special school so that they do not lose contact with developments in special schools. Indeed, if this link is fostered, it could provide important back-up for the designated unit with opportunities for interchange of staff.

There are important points to be considered in developing designated units in ordinary schools. A host school should have good standing in its local community and be making reasonable provision for the individual differences of its pupils; teachers, governors and parents should have an accepting attitude to handicapped pupils; it must be possible to provide access for unit pupils to each department of the school; adequate health and social service support should be available; it should be possible to provide at least two adequate, separate teaching spaces for the unit together with accommodation for support staff; there should be arrangements for the additional clerical work generated by the unit; suitably qualified teachers must be available to at least the standard of a similar special school together with adequate assistance with general duties and the staffing, capitation and equipment must be above the normal allocation to the host school. Great care will be necessary in reaching a decision about the size of the roll in the designated unit and it must be restricted to a level which does not create an abnormal situation for the ordinary pupils in the host school. The total staffing of school and unit should be considered to ensure that it is generous enough to support the interaction noted above as a mark of a mature situation and required by the Education Act 1981. Most important of all, there should be a planned policy on interaction for pupils and staff which is clear in its objectives and operation and is known by all concerned.

Providing appropriate education for pupils with special needs *not* determined by the LEA in statements will form the larger part of special education in the ordinary schools and new standards of teaching and monitoring will extend school responsibilities. Added to the task in some schools will be the responsibilities generated by designated classes or units for pupils whose special educational needs *are* determined in a statement by the LEA. Organizing inter-action within the school, extended contributions from members of supportive services and the clerical work demanded by the new responsibilities will generate management problems in comprehensive schools and in the larger primary schools. Timetabling designated unit pupils into ordinary classes, reviewing their progress and advising their ordinary teachers, making arrangements for multi-professional review when required, responding to approaches from their parents about their education and developing that part of their special education provided in the designated unit will create new professional tasks within the school. The total of these duties, in both extent and complexity, form a daunting task and it is doubtful if an existing organization based upon "slow learners" or "remedial" departments will prove adequate in the new situation. A fresh approach is required. The starting point could be the concept of all-embracing special education in the school centred upon the specialist teachers in the designated unit but with implications and involvements reaching into every department or class in the school and making a contribution to overall school policy. To direct this a head of special education will be necessary. She will not head a department as such, nor lead a faculty, but her area of influence will range over the whole school where the pupils for whom she is responsible will create problems for her teacher colleagues. The group of special education teachers will form the support base on which the head of SE may draw in arranging advice for colleagues and special teaching for pupils at any level and they should be the start of a resource facility in the school. But more is required if the new situation is to be fully exploited. The head of special education should lead a working group in the school which includes an interested teacher from every department or faculty in secondary school or from each year level in a large primary school. Each would become the point of interaction between their colleagues and the working group bringing suggestions, ideas and problems for discussion. They would identify information and support required by their colleagues, consult on curriculum and teaching methods for children with special needs and when necessary secure inputs to department, faculty or year-group meetings. At the same time each member of the working group would participate in the formulation of school policy relative to pupils with special needs for submission to accademic board or staff council as appropriate. In time there would be at least one member of every section of the school well informed about the place of special education in the school and the teaching of children with special needs in her own area of curricula. A later development would be to train interested teachers from the subject areas of the school in special teaching and to formulate a role for them in the resource facility so that it may become a resource centre drawing from and contributing to every area of the school. To be effective in her leadership role the head of special education must be more than a specialist teacher of children with special needs. She must have broad interests and a wide background in education, be interested in and contribute to the wider activities of the school, while in professional competence and personal qualities she must stand equal with other senior colleagues in the school. It would be appropriate to write such a person into the school senior management team at a level just below that of the deputy headteacher.

One other development in ordinary schools requires consideration. It is what might be termed a "neighbourhood" policy in which children with special educational needs determined by the LEA attend their local school and arrangements are made to meet their needs in that school. What is often overlooked is that in the normal run of things a local primary school would never have more than two or three pupils with special needs determined by the LEA and, even for physically handicapped pupils, the alterations needed to enable the school to meet their needs are relatively simple. What is required, though, is assurance that medical needs can be provided for from local community services with adequate special education advice from appropriately qualified and experienced peripatetic advisory teachers. This type of provision is most suitable for small primary schools. At secondary level school populations naturally concentrate and this also applies to pupils with special needs; here a basic unit to provide in-school support may be more appropriate. Another feature of the arrangement is its apparent suitability in rural areas where school populations are thinly spread.

DEVELOPMENT IN SPECIAL SCHOOLS

Special schools have a long history as a means of providing education for handicapped pupils in Britain. In its evidence to the Warnock Committee the largest education authority, ILEA, affirmed that ". . . in many respects, the special school represents a highly developed technique of positive discrimination", and the weight of evidence supported their continuation alongside movement into ordinary schools. The committee concluded that there was a continuing role for special schools in the new system of special education, and the 1981 Act secures their future. Nevertheless change is inevitable. The prevailing ethos which questions the wisdom of separating handicapped pupils from their fellows, the extension of provision for special education in ordinary schools, and the predicted fall in the school population in the 1980s will threaten some individual special schools and require adaption to a new situation for those which remain. Change will, however, be gradual. The school population does not reach its predicted low until the end of the decade and the move into ordinary schools makes demands on training and resources unlikely to be met in the short term. As demand for teachers falls off in special schools their skill and experience will be in demand for the designated situations in the ordinary schools, two features which should be considered by those who plan the changes.

There is also the possibility of further changes in the pattern of disabilities which affect children. Extension and improvement in genetic counselling, more sophisticated diagnosis in early pregnancy allied to termination, improved obstetrics and pre- and post-natal care may both reduce handicaps and change their pattern. Against this must be set the current run-down of the health and social services which results from government policy of reduced expenditure allied to the effect of inflation; the lowering in extent and quality of the school meal service for similar reasons; and the scale of unemployment which could lead to the reappearance of nutritional diseases to the elimination of which the school meals service made a significant contribution.

The effect of the changes on the special schools can be predicted with reasonable confidence. There will be fewer special schools; either their rolls will be smaller or their catchment areas wider; they will, in general, provide for pupils with serious disabilities or with complex combinations of disability; their intake will change, reflecting the broader groupings of special educational needs; they will require more specialized curricula and teaching methods; and they will be in grave danger of becoming isolated in the system of education. These are the changes to which special schools must respond and adapt.

Schools and school rolls

Because there will be fewer special schools the location of those which remain will be critical. Links with families, transport of pupils to schools, input from health and social services will all require evaluation in relation to school location. The size of roll will raise questions of curriculum validity in many schools. Yet this must be seen against the changes in intake, for the curriculum may be more circumscribed by the needs of seriously and multiply handicapped pupils. These factors may be offset if the broader grouping of needs results in a lifting of school roll, though this itself may reintroduce the question of curriculum viability. Questions of curriculum viability may also be affected by interaction with ordinary schools, discussed previously. Some of these questions will raise the issue of the extent to which designated units are capable of providing education for seriously or multiply handicapped pupils. At present there is little experience on which to base answers to such questions, but conditions may require continuous evaluation of them as experience extends. In rural areas there may be an early, forced choice between the alternatives of designated units or boarding provision.

Serious and Complex Disabilities

It is an open question whether providing for a limited range of complex or serious disabilities is a more difficult task than educating the same children in a school where the other children range to the near-normal. The only certain thing is that both problems are difficult, though different. The limited population of the school will allow teachers to concentrate on the specialized curricula and teaching methods required by a narrow range of serious or complex handicaps. Curriculum objectives will be more easily defined, equipment and materials more easily related to the task, method more carefully shaped to the needs of the pupils, support inputs more specifically related to needs and the purpose of the school explained to parents and the community with greater clarity. On the other hand, deviation from the ordinary school will increase. The balance of education and care in the schools will change; consequently the role of teachers will be subtly affected; educational progress by the children may be relatively slow, requiring finer definitions of sub-goals or objectives or the postulation of learning objectives over an unrealistic period of time; while teaching and learning situations form a smaller proportion of the school day. The needs of the pupils may dictate a pattern of school day and school year which introduces another deviation from the normal pattern of schools. In many schools medical and para-medical needs will impose greater constraints on education, affecting more pupils and requiring more of their time away from the classroom, and absence through illness or hospitalization will more frequently interupt the slow educational progress.

In the above situation it will not be possible to balance work with seriously handicapped pupils by work with those less handicapped with near-normal educational progress, for the latter group will not be in the school. Against this, the need to develop new methods through experimental teaching will attract some teachers and for them provide a balance. Others may derive personal satisfaction from the challenge presented by the children, or from the commitment required for work with seriously handicapped pupils, to a degree which balances the slow gradient of educational progress by the children. As parents of children with serious disabilities are usually closely involved with schools, some teachers may derive satisfaction from the closer interaction with families which is made possible and so balance the constraints. If the broader concept of special educational needs prevails some special schools may admit a wider range of disabilities than at present so that some variety in the teachers' work may come from working in different areas of the school rather than at different levels. Similarly, teachers who work with seriously handicapped children (i.e., those currently designated ESN(S)) often perceive physical and personality differences in their pupils which are not obvious to visitors and thus they enjoy a variety and richness in the child group which is denied to outsiders. This may operate more widely in the special schools of the future.

Serious questions arise from the above considerations. Will sufficient teachers be motivated to remain in the special schools of the future? Or will there be a tendency to desert them for the nearer normal educational satisfactions to be had in designated units, or in special classes? Will teachers remaining in the special schools lose contact with educational expectations? Will the motivation which keeps them there be sufficient to maintain educational initiative against the weight of care and medicine? Is it a "good" thing, in terms of both professional and personal well-being, that a teacher should remain for long periods in a situation of severe disability and extremely slow or deviant educational progress? At present there can be no certain answers to these questions which can only be resolved on the basis of experience. Some attempt is necessary, therefore, to guard against the dangers of extreme separation from the mainstream of education.

One way to resolve the question of separation would be to insist that, eventually, all children with special needs should be educated in suitably organized situations within ordinary schools. That would certainly resolve some staff problems, even if pupil interaction were minimal. At present such a notion would have little support among parents, teachers or public though time and experience may lead to change. The Warnock Report suggested that some special schools should become "centres of excellence" and support for ordinary schools. The chosen schools might well resolve their problems through this development but it is difficult to see how they could support ordinary schools across the widened deviance gap, except, perhaps, through interaction with a designated unit. Another approach would be to retain a wider population in the special school which should be closely associated with ordinary schools and develop maximum interaction with them, so that, where appropriate, special school pupils could be taught in the ordinary school. To be effective this needs good design in a "campus" setting, is more suitable for certain handicaps, and might be ruled out in urban areas through difficulties in obtaining suitable building sites. When properly planned the arrangement does work well but it is doubtful if it could ever solve the whole of the problem. Perhaps a better approach would be to accept the forecast developments and consider how the obvious disadvantages of the new special schools could be reduced.

SPECIAL-ORDINARY SCHOOL INTERACTION

A radical approach to ordinary and special school interaction must break down the present isolation of special schools in the system in a way which will override the greater "distance" which may develop in the future and at the same time prevent the isolation of special school teachers from their colleagues in designated units and on the general staff of ordinary schools. It should also create a situation in which teachers working with severely handicapped pupils in the special schools find it easier than at present to maintain contact with mainstream education through balance and variety in their teaching experience. To achieve the objective it may be necessary to abandon current ideas about the staffing of special schools and think instead of staffing special education. Each designated unit in an ordinary school should be closely associated with an appropriate special school. Normally there would be a trinity of primary unit, secondary unit and special school. The staffing of the units should be handled in the special education branch of the LEA in the same manner as the staffing of the special school and the head of that school should have a special relationship with the units. All staff of special schools and designated units should be regarded as special education branch staff and teachers should be able to interchange between the three situations without any obstacles in relation to scale posts which they may hold. It would be advisable to have a single special education adviser or inspector responsible for the group of school and units in order to control and regulate staff interaction. There would also be a need to involve the headteachers of the host ordinary schools, for their schools would be affected by special education interchange and they should clear any arrangements before they operate. Meetings between the heads and teachers of the three schools/units should be held from time to time to exchange ideas and discuss common problems while the host school inspectors and the SE inspectors might participate in some of the meetings. These arrangements would ensure adequate discussion of policy at school level and create valuable insight in top management. Staff interaction between special school and units would be by mutual agreement which also took account of the effects on pupils. But it would be necessary to establish that the interaction was a condition of the employment of teachers. The interaction between special school and units should also relate to interaction between the units and their host schools. Thus teachers from the special school, while working on the staff of a unit, would also participate in some teaching in the ordinary classes of the host school. Much thought and experiment would be required to develop this or a similar system of interchange but, properly developed, it could rid the system of isolation and bring special education as fully as possible into the mainstream of education. For the teachers, it would resolve many of the problems of balanced experience noted above to the extent that, in a few years time, a teacher aspiring to senior responsibility in special education could be expected to have experience of teaching in special schools and designated situations and to have kept a continuing contact with mainstream teaching.

Boarding special schools will present particular problems in the development of interaction similar to that outlined above. It may be that the need to place children away from home may overlap other educational needs so that the population of residential schools will be less concentrated at the extreme of disability. But the overall need to promote interaction and reduce the isolation of teachers will remain. Where boarding schools are within the area of the LEA then interaction with local day schools should not present too much difficulty. But where a boarding school is in the area of another LEA the situation becomes more complicated and calls for good cooperation between the LEAs and their schools. In this situation there will be advantages in the boarding school providing day places for local pupils who require special school placement. Here again, good cooperation is necessary and has the advantage of making maximum use of existing resources. Considerations such as these should form part of regional planning in special education.

The problem of the relationship between the remaining special schools and the mainstream system requires continuing careful thought and must be closely watched as the new system develops. Many of the suggestions made in the Warnock Report are fine so long as the special schools remain as they are now. But the committee appears to have paid too little attention to the effect on special schools of their suggestions for the movement of special education into ordinary schools. In teaching methods, curriculum, pace of learning, balance of education against care and post-school prospects for the pupils the difference between ordinary and special schools may be qualitative rather than quantitative. Consequently the sharing of resources and teaching *by the pupils*; the development of common aspects of curriculum; and short-term provision for pupils on the roll of ordinary schools may present more problems than have been anticipated. If the move to ordinary schools is successfully completed, even social interaction between pupils may need careful preparation and organization. A simple example highlights the situation. Once a designated unit is operating in an ordinary school, what is the point of pupils visiting from a special school to participate in part of the ordinary school curriculum? Surely in most cases of this kind such pupils would be better placed in the designated unit. Only the fact that a suitable designated unit was not available could justify the initial arrangement. If the point made in this paragraph appears exaggerated, consider the conditions for placement in a special school identified in the Warnock Report:

> 1. Children with severe or complex physical, sensory or intellectual disabilities who require special facilities, teaching methods or expertise that it would be impracticable to provide in ordinary schools.
> 2. Children with severe emotional or behavioural disorders who have very great difficulty in forming relationships with others or whose behaviour is so extreme or unpredictable that it causes severe disruption in an ordinary school or inhibits the educational progress of other children.
> 3. Children with less severe disabilities, often in combination, who despite special help do not perform well in an ordinary school and are more likely to thrive in the more intimate communal and educational setting of a special school. (DES, 1978)[3].

Note, too, that when places in designated units are widely available only the extremes of the above groups will be in special schools. This is not an argument against the movement of as much special education as possible into properly-designated situations in ordinary schools. It is, rather, a case for a much more careful and realistic look at what the move implies for the remaining special schools.

THE SCHOOL CURRICULUM

This is not the place for a detailed discussion of the development of curricula in special education, for that would require a book in itself. It is necessary, however, to identify problems and indicate broadly the direction in which schools should advance. The Warnock Report identified certain weaknesses: a preoccupation with teaching methods at the expense of consideration of objectives, materials or learning experiences; inadequate attention to experiences relating to post-school life; too little attention to planned programmes and their effectiveness. Evidence suggested that special schools underestimated the ability of pupils at all levels and considered that the curricula should be broadened in many directions (11.8). The committee found evidence to substantiate these points but they also found schools providing excellent curricula (11.13). The situation is clear. Excellent special schools exist but are a minority in the system, so the problem is that of bringing all schools nearer to the level of the best. Wherever curriculum quality was high two main factors emerged: well-defined guidelines for each area of the curriculum; and programmes for individual children with well-defined, short-term goals within a general plan. Other marks of quality were continuity of approach, consistency among staff, agreed goals, and close work with the supporting services.

To improve curricula in the special schools and other situations which will provide special education it is essential that planning should start with the children and their needs, add to that a knowledge of their home and neighbourhood circumstances, and consider the demands that may face the pupils as young adults. Objectives should be selected which cover emotional, social, intellectual and physical development and learning. They must be practicable and realistically related to the children for whom they are intended with the steps by which they are to be attained carefully worked out; and there must be an organized means of judging whether or not the objectives have been attained. Clear knowledge of objectives and an intimate knowledge of the pupils will shape the choice of experiences, materials and teaching and learning methods to be utilized by the teacher in her work. The whole of the curriculum process and content will require regular and continuing review if high quality is to be achieved and maintained. Much work will be required in curriculum development, and for children with special educational needs most of it must be school based so that development and implementation go hand in hand. This kind of work is rarely allowed for when the staffing levels of schools are considered; it may become necessary to do so, not only for schools but also for designated units. Special attention will have to be given to the problems faced by children with special needs when they leave school, to vocational guidance, career and consumer education and to health education in all its aspects. This part of curriculum requires a firm, practical base in real experience outside the school.

FURTHER EDUCATION

Further education is an area almost totally unexplored for young people with special needs. Its problems are relatively uncharted and this is surely partly responsible for the unemployment and underemployment of handicapped young people. Naturally, education for the 16-19 age group must face the fact that for many of those with special needs, the objectives of further education must include many which normal pupils would already have achieved during the years of statutory education. Moreover, there is a direct relationship between what can actually be achieved in FE and the quality of the curriculum to which the students have previously been subjected.

The ordinary schools obviously have an immediate role to play in the education of the 16-19 age group through their sixth forms. The development of designated special units in secondary schools would enable more students with special needs to stay on in sixth forms and their presence might make it more possible for students from special schools to join the sixth-form group. Realistically, however, for all except an able minority, the development of less academic sixth-form work is required. This is anyway a current trend for "normal" students in sixth forms.

Nevertheless, what little experience there has been in colleges of further education does suggest that they are able to provide courses adapted to the vocational requirements of handicapped students, and to provide social development courses for students who need time to achieve maturity. It might be noted that teachers experienced with handicapped senior pupils would be suited for this work, and might become available if the scale of special school work were reduced. These teachers would require initiation into FE work, and selected members of the college staffs will require courses introducing them to special education. In the latter courses a major contribution should be from the Advisory and Support Services in special education. There should also be close association of the A&SS and the AEO/SE in the development of further education for young people with special educational needs. As the work develops there should be continued involvement of special education advisers or inspectors and the responsibility requires clear definition.

Mentally handicapped young people entering senior training centres will have their educational needs provided for by the teachers to be appointed to the centres. Rather different contributions will be required for mentally or physically handicapped adults in training centres or day care centres. The need here is not for continuous, developmental curricula but for leisure and cultural activities which capture the interests of the adults and give some pattern and purpose to their lives. This contribution is more appropriate for adult education, and where this is organized separately from FE the contribution would be more suited to the organization of an Adult Education Institute. The institutes could also develop another contribution to special education.

It will be recalled that in considering pre-school education parent education was accorded considerable importance in the work of the home teacher. Her work could be supported by adult education courses designed for parents of handicapped children. Other general courses might attempt to disseminate knowledge of handicap and the place of handicapped people in society at the level of popular information with the objective of contributing to the improvement of community attitudes to disabled members. Adult education could also do more to inform handicapped persons and their families about the support that is available from public sources and voluntary bodies and the manner in which the support may be secured. There is also the problem of hospitalized and home-bound adults. During their school years the hospital schools or groups and the home tuition service provide for children with these special educational needs but the situation of adults is not so clearly covered. There is reason to believe that many adults in the above situation are under-occupied, lack intellectual or cultural activities and may be downright lonely. Many voluntary bodies do what they can, often with financial support from public funds. But there is a case for more serious consideration of the role of the education service and, if developed, it would be an appropriate task for special adult education.

The DES is currently consulting LEAs and other bodies about the whole of Further Education and the consultative document places special stress on the provision of F.E. for young people with special educational needs.

SUMMARY

Pre-school education should be a growth area in special education. The intervention of home teachers may arrest the development of some special educational needs and prevent others from arising. To do this parents must be seen as the child's first educators and to involve them is part of the home teacher's task. The work requires the support of other services and voluntary organizations.

Once the child is in school early detection of emerging special educational needs has high priority so that early provision may keep the child in mainstream education or provide appropriate special education as soon as possible. Improved teacher training should increase the quality of detection but to be certain of identifying children with special educational needs, an annual survey of the school population between 7 and 8 years of age is necessary. Most children requiring special education will receive it in ordinary schools—some in special classes organized by head-teachers. For children with special educational needs determined by a statement LEAs will organize "designated" special classes or units in selected ordinary schools. Points to be considered in setting up these classes have been described. They require the same staffing and facilities as similar special schools, they must review pupils annually in the same manner and interact with both the host school and an appropriate special school. It is suggested that secondary schools and large primary schools should have a head of special education. She should be responsible for all SE in the school and lead a working party which would include special education teachers and a representative from each department in the school. An important task is the development of a resources centre which will serve all special needs wherever they occur in the school.

Special schools are to continue but will face change as a result of the movement of special education into ordinary schools and the predicted fall in the schools population. Some will close. The remainder may be smaller or have wider catchment areas. The children in them will be those with severe or multiple special educational needs and the schools may need to become more specialized in meeting their needs. The balance of care to education will change, educational progress may be slow, and there will be more intrusions into the normal pattern of education. The special schools may become more separate from ordinary schools and their teachers may become isolated to a greater extent than at present. It is thought that some of the discussion about interaction between special and ordinary schools does not take sufficient account of impending changes in special schools. A suggestion is made that the staffing of special schools should be abandoned and replaced by a unified system of staffing areas of special education, regarding special schools and grouped designated units as one staffing area with regular and regulated interchanges of teachers. A special education inspector responsible for the group would regulate the interchange in cooperation with the headteachers of the schools and the teachers in charge of the designated units. The objective should be that a special education teacher in mid-career should have taught in both special schools and units and have maintained some teaching contact with mainstream education.

Some weaknesses in the curriculum in special schools have been identified. There is a need for improvement in the curriculum though some schools are achieving a high standard. Good curriculum is identified with well-defined guidelines for each area of curriculum and programmes for individual children with well-defined short-term goals within a general plan. Other features are continuity of approach, consistency among staff, agreed goals and close work with the supporting services. The curriculum should become more concerned with objectives which are practicable and relevant for the children and related to the demands which children will face as young adults. The curriculum for school leavers should also relate in a practical way to conditions outside the school.

Further education is regarded as being relatively unexplored for young people with special educational needs and is identified as an area where development is urgently required. There should be more opportunity for students with special needs to stay on in sixth forms, which may have to develop less academic courses. Work in colleges of further education also requires expansion at vocational level, and in general courses aimed at personal and social development. There should be contributions to development from special education inspectors or advisers and training for lecturers will be necessary. Teachers in senior training centres will provide continued education for mentally handicapped young people entering the centres. Adults in senior training and day care centres, in hospital or home bound have special needs which should be the concern of adult education. Courses for parents of pre-school handicapped children would be appropriate for adult education and could support the work of the home teachers. Other courses should have the objective of making sure that the support available for the handicapped is widely known and should attempt to improve the general attitudes to handicapped persons in the community.

The point is made that the changes envisaged will be gradual and there is time for planning an efficient transition; for instance, teachers experienced with children in special schools might move into designated units or further education as one field contracts and the others expand. Some in-service training will be required to support the transition.

NOTES AND REFERENCES

1. DEPARTMENT OF EDUCATION AND SCIENCE (1978), *Special Educational Needs*, HMSO, pp80-93.
2. DES, *op.cit.*, p56.
3. DES, *op.cit.*, p123.

6

CHANGING SPECIAL EDUCATION

WHERE ARE WE NOW?

The early chapters of this book attempted to show the kind of changes which have taken place in special education. Extension of the legally-defined categories of handicapped children failed to generate the flexibility in schools which was recognized as necessary by their parents and by teachers and this remained true even when a degree of informality was introduced into the system. Associated with this was growing dissatisfaction with the medical model which prevailed in special education. Disability of mind or body; treatment as a concept dominating a development, educational process; and a system of assessment for special education heavily influenced by professionals neither engaged in nor experienced in the teaching and education of the children being assessed; these factors also contributed to dissatisfaction. The response was a combined pressure for multidisciplinary approaches to assessment with the emphasis on education and a system based upon a description of the special educational needs of children to which could be related the proposals for their education. Other factors were also at work. The importance of the first years of a child's life was clearly demonstrated and with it the unique position of the parents as educators in those years, as well as the value of good quality pre-school education. Meanwhile a new democracy was abroad which emphasized the rights of individuals to information and it was reflected in the parent movement, in particular in the rights of the parents of children with disabilities not only to be informed, but to be consulted and fully involved in any assessment of their child's needs and proposals for the child's special education. As segregation in secondary education has generally faded with the growth of comprehensive secondary schools, so the pressure increased for the education of more children with disabilities within the ordinary schools in preference to education in the separate special schools. At the same time, it was noted, the greater part of public expenditure on special education found its outlet in the expansion of special school provision which absorbed most of the output of teachers specially trained to work with children with special needs. The opportunities afforded by legislation for the education of handicapped children in ordinary schools were not exploited. And, perhaps even more important, where good provision existed in ordinary schools it more often resulted from the initiative of the teachers concerned than from positive and purposeful planning by the local education authorities. By the end of the 1970s there were still pupils waiting for places in the special schools considered necessary for their education. But far greater in numbers, and not necessarily less at risk, were the children in ordinary schools with learning, behavioural or other difficulties for whom no adequate special teaching was provided. Ironically, though thin on the ground, the good situations noted above were adequate demonstration that the needs of most of these children could be appropriately and efficiently provided for within ordinary schools. Through all this there was increasing questioning of the education offered in schools, particularly in terms of the basic knowledge and life skills required for participation in society as adult members and workers. Special education was not exempt from this, and , inevitably, the weight fell on the special schools. It was realized that many children with special needs, because of the operation of those needs, could not be expected to achieve the normal goals of school leavers within the years of statutory education. The response was a demand for better provision for children with special needs in further education—an area found to be almost wholly unexploited so far as the needs of these young people were concerned.

THE WARNOCK REPORT[1]

The culmination of the above pressures and changes saw the appointment of the Warnock Committee to which constant reference has been made. The priority areas of the committee's report are now summarized so that readers may compare them with the legislation in the Education Act 1981. The report established there areas of first priority:

1. Provision for children under 5 with special educational needs.

This was to include the recognition and involvement of parents as the first educators of their children; substantial expansion of nursery education for all children; extension of peripatetic teaching services to all types of disability in young children; provision of professional help and advice from supporting services, including the proposed special education advisory and support service, to playgroups, opportunity groups, day nurseries and, above all, parents.

2. Provision for young people over 16 with special educational needs. This includes: more opportunity to continue education at school or in further education and to receive careers guidance; variety of provision in FE ordinary courses and special courses with a special FE unit in each region; a specifically educational element in adult training centres and day centres; and necessary financial support to enable young people with special needs to undertake courses of further and higher education.

3. Teacher training should include: a special education element in all courses of initial teacher training, short courses of one week (or equivalent) duration on special educational needs to be taken by the great majority of serving teachers within a few years; one year full-time (or equivalent) courses leading to a qualification in special education for teachers with a defined responsibility for children with special educational needs; other short courses on different aspects of special education; and the promotion of research and development to increase knowledge and understanding of different aspects of special education.

In addition, among over 200 recommendations, the report recommended changes in assessment procedures leading to a statement of special educational need, a clear definition of the circumstances identifying special education, and described the variety of special educational situations necessary to meet them as discussed in earlier chapters. It recommended the appointment of a 'named person' for all children with special educational needs.

THE EDUCATION ACT 1981 (SPECIAL EDUCATIONAL NEEDS)

The Act establishes that a child has a special educational need if he or she has a learning difficulty significantly greater than the majority of children of that age or a disability which prevents the use of educational facilities of a kind generally provided in the schools for children of that age. Special educational provision is educational provision which is additional to, or otherwise different from, the educational provision made generally for children the same age as the child concerned in schools maintained by the LEA. It is the duty of the LEA to identify and assess children over 2 years of age in their area who may have special educational needs. In doing this they must seek medical, psychological and educational advice. Where it decides it is necessary, the LEA must determine the special education to be provided by making a statement of special educational needs which must also set out the proposals for meeting them. Parents dissatisfied with the LEA decision may appeal, first to the local appeal committee then, if necessary, to the Secretary of State. Where the LEA does *not* make a statement after assessment, dissatisfied parents may appeal to the Secretary of State. Requests from parents for the assessment of their children must be granted by the LEA unless they are unreasonable. It is also the duty of the LEA to inform parents of the intention to assess their child's needs, to name an officer who will give them further information, and to make sure that they know of their rights to present evidence to the assessment and, if necessary, appeal against its outcome. A 'named person' will be appointed to support the parents of children for whom the LEA has made a statement of special educational needs.

The LEA has a duty to educate in ordinary schools those children for whom it has made a statement providing that appropriate special education is available compatible with the efficient education of other children and the efficient use of resources and that the views of parents have been considered. Headteachers and governors of ordinary schools have a duty to ensure that children with special educational needs participate in school activities with pupils without such needs, that the teachers who teach them are aware of their needs; and that all teachers are aware of the importance of identifying and providing for such pupils. The LEA must keep its arrangements for special education under review and the needs of pupils for whom the authority has made a statement must be reviewed annually. Pupils in special schools when the Act operates will be regarded as being subject to a statement and the education provided must be continued until their needs are assessed as laid down in the Act.

Special schools are to continue and the Secretary of State will make regulations defining conditions for recognition of a special school. Similar regulations are to be made establishing conditions for the recognition of independent schools as special schools. Only schools meeting the conditions and approved by the Secretary of State may be used by LEAs for the placement of children with special educational needs. LEAs wishing to close special schools must give notice to parents of children, other LEAs with children in the school and any interested bodies. The proposal and any objections must go to the Secretary of State whose approval is necessary before the LEA may cease to maintain the school.

A COMPARISON

To what extent does the legislation in the Education Act 1981 incorporate the recommendations made in the Warnock Report, about which members of the committee were unanimous and which was widely welcomed by professionals in special education and the parents of children with special educational needs? A short answer is: to a very limited extent. An editorial in the journal *Special Education*[2] puts the point well:

> The bill has been described by Mr Neil Kinnock as "a Michelin guide to nowhere". Perhaps it would be fairer to say, as he did in the same second reading debate in the Commons on February 2, that, like Brighton pier, "it is good as far as it goes but it is not much of a way to get to France". If, for France, are substituted the Warnock Report's three priority areas of provision for the under fives, the over 16s and teacher training, plus more water-tight safeguards about the quality of special education provision in ordinary schools, the description is apt.

There is nothing in the Act which will increase pressure for extended and improved special education in the pre-school years, though the right of the LEA to operate there is made somewhat clearer, while further education and teacher training receive no attention. The failure to establish any minimum standards for the provision of special education in ordinary schools contrasts mark-edly with the stated intention to establish conditions to regulate both LEA special schools and independent schools intending to admit children with special educational needs. The contrast is marked because it appears in an Act one intention of which is that more special education should be provided within ordinary schools. Of course these omissions arise from the decision of the govern-ment that no additional resources would be made available for implementation of the Education Act. For the same reason the definitions of learning difficulties and special educational provision are left vague. Adoption of the definitions recommended in the Warnock Report (see Chapter 4) would have related the definitions to resources and teachers and probably could not be contemplated in view of the decision on resources. Unfortunately the vagueness will have other effects. The definitions in the Act relate a child's needs to the generality of others of the same age in the locality and the same is true of definitions of special education provision. Nothing is as effective as generalization for promoting irresolvable argument, so it may be that the Act will generate misunderstanding between parents and LEAs. But more important, the approach abandons any attempt by central government to secure equality of special educational opportunity throughout the different regions of England and Wales. Similarly, the Act lacks any indication of an understanding of the close cooperation between the public services which has been shown to be necessary if special education is to be extended into ordinary schools and improved in quality both there and in special schools. And there is no concept of the immense task which faces initial and in-service training if properly-prepared teachers are to be available for both tasks with adequate support from experienced Advisory and Support Services in special education.

It could be argued, of course, that the government was a prisoner of economic circumstances which made the allocation of additional resources impossible. This is not the place to argue out such a proposition, but even if it is accepted much of the Education Act 1981 does not make good sense. Presumably supporters of economic determinism would argue that in the circumstances the Act is intended only to initiate change, for the Warnock Committee saw its recommendations as long term with twenty years advanced as the time necessary for full implementation. But, to continue the illustration quoted above, if Brighton pier does not extend to France, any intention to make it reach there will be assisted if those responsible know which part of the French coast it is intended to reach. Apply this to the Education Act 1981 and its weakness becomes evident. It is entirely short term, it reaches nowhere, and, of itself, it gives those who must operate it no idea of where it is intended to lead. In practical terms this means that development beyond the Act is left to the initiative of local education authorities until a subsequent government rises to the challenge and sets a course. Unfortunately for children with special educational needs, this means that the quality of their special education may well be determined by the place in which they live and attend school.

TO WHAT PURPOSE?

In the present circumstances it is important that those concerned with special education—parents, teachers, supporting professionals, care workers, administrators, advisers and members of education authorities—should maintain a sense of purpose which goes beyond immediate short-term considerations. The children described in Chapter 1 are typical. In future others like them will have similar special needs and they, too, will require special education appropriate to their needs. But their special education should be more than appropriate: it should also be of good quality and it should be so as a result of planning with purpose rather than fortuitous circumstances. It cannot, at present, be confidently asserted that every child who needs it is receiving special education which reflects the above qualities, and indeed the education of some may lack all three. So there is no shortage of work to be done at all levels.

Achieving appropriateness and good quality as a result of planning is more important than the place in which the education is delivered. Nevertheless, the current ethos which demands that wherever possible children with special needs should be educated in ordinary schools and interact with children without such needs is correct and it is right that the principle should be encompassed in legislation. Experience has shown, however, that there is much which may "slip away" between legislation and practice and this time it must not be allowed to happen. Nor should it be overlooked that among the most disadvantaged children in our schools are those in the ordinary schools who have special educational needs about which little is being done. Consequently, one of the first moves in ordinary schools should be to make proper arrangements for the education of pupils with special needs *who are already in the schools*. In no circumstances should the needs of such pupils be ignored in premature attempts to place in ordinary schools pupils with more severe special needs.

The Education Act 1981, notwithstanding its limitations, does allow a start to be made on implementing the broader concept of special education. It removes the concept of disabilities of mind or body, ends the idea of special educational treatment, and abolishes the legal categories of handicapped children. These are essential requirements, but of themselves they will not convert the concept of broader areas of special educational needs into the central feature of special education in action. For that changed attitudes are essential. Handicapped people must be seen as in full membership of the community, the notion of a "dole" for the handicapped should disappear and be replaced by opportunities for them to contribute to society on the basis of their abilities, as all citizens should. The concept of equality, of treating people alike, should give way to the concept of equity, of treating people according to their needs. No longer should a single disability be regarded as an all-round handicap or an obtrusive one as a sign that the person has fewer emotional or social needs than others. Teachers in ordinary schools must lose their fear of children with special needs and those in special schools learn to admit that for some of their pupils the ordinary school might be a more appropriate place for their special education. Educationists, careers officers, and employers must seek new opportunities for young people in further education, in training and in employment. Parents of normal children must lose the fear that the presence of children with special needs in the school will be a disadvantage for their own children. Instead they should use their collective power to insist that the local education authority makes facilities available to meet the needs of *all* children in the schools. These are the attitudes necessary to make a reality of the broader concept of special education and it is to the Warnock Report that parents and educators must look for their lead.

NOTES AND REFERENCES

1. DEPARTMENT OF EDUCATION AND SCIENCE (1978), *Special Educational Needs*, HMSO, pp 336-7.
2. *Special Education*, vol. 8, No. 1, March 1981.

APPENDIX 1

Categories of Handicapped Pupils

The categories below are as set out in *Handicapped Pupils and Special Schools Regulations 1959*, as amended 1962. The figures in brackets indicate the maximum class sizes allowed until replaced by a recommended pupil-teacher ratio in 1973. First figure class size: second figure pupil-teacher ratio.

Blind pupils, that is to say, pupils who have no sight or whose sight is or is likely to become so defective that they require education by methods not involving the use of sight. (15. 1:6)

Partially sighted pupils, that is to say, pupils who by reason of defective vision cannot follow the normal regime of ordinary schools without detriment to their sight or to their educational development, but can be educated by special methods involving the use of sight. (15. 1:8.5)

Deaf pupils, that is to say, pupils with impaired hearing who require education by methods suitable for pupils with little or no naturally acquired speech or language. (10. 1:6.5 primary, 1:5.5 secondary)

Partially hearing pupils, that is to say, pupils with impaired hearing whose development of speech and language, even if retarded, is following a normal pattern, and who require for their education special arrangements or facilities though not necessarily all the educational methods used for deaf pupils. (10. 1:6.5 primary, 1:5.5 secondary)

Educationally subnormal pupils, that is to say, pupils who, by reason of limited ability or other conditions resulting in educational retardation, require some specialized form of education wholly or partly in substitution for the education normally given in ordinary schools. (20. ESN(S) 1:8.5, ESN(M) 1:11)

Epileptic pupils, that is to say, pupils who by reason of epilepsy cannot be educated under the normal regime of ordinary schools without detriment to themselves or other pupils. (20.1:9)

Maladjusted pupils, that is to say, pupils who show evidence of emotional instability or psychological disturbance and require special educational treatment in order to effect their personal, social or educational readjustment. (15. 1:6)

Physically handicapped pupils, that is to say, pupils not suffering solely from a defect of sight or hearing who by reason of disease or crippling defect cannot, without detriment to their health or educational development, be satisfactorily educated under the normal regime of ordinary schools. (20. 1:7)

Pupils suffering from speech defect, that is to say, pupils who on account of defect or lack of speech not due to deafness require special educational treatment. (as per deaf pupils)

Delicate pupils, that is to say, pupils not falling under any other category in this regulation, who by reason of impaired physical condition need a change of environment or cannot, without risk to their health or educational development, be educated under the normal regime of ordinary schools. (30. 1:8)

APPENDIX 2

Useful Addresses

Advisory Centre for Education, 18 Victoria Park Square, London E2.

Association of Professions for the Mentally Handicapped, 126 Albert Street, London NW1

Association of Workers for Maladjusted Children, New Barnes School, Church Lane, Toddington, Glos.

British Association of Teachers of the Deaf, 20 Devonshire Road, Bolton, Lancs.

British Dyslexia Association, 18 The Circus, Bath BA1 2ET.

British Epilepsy Association, 140 Holland Park Avenue, London W11 4UF.

Centre on Environment for the Handicapped, 126 Albert Street, London NW1

Child Poverty Action Group, 1 Macklin Street, London WC2.

College of Teachers of the Blind, Royal School for the Blind, Church Road North, Wavertree, Liverpool L15 6TQ.

Confederation for the Advancement of State Education:
> *England:* 1 Windermere Avenue, Wembley, Middlesex HA9 8SH.
> *Scotland:* The Old Schoolhouse, Inverchaolain, Toward, Argyll.

Disabled Living Foundation, 346 Kensington High Street, London W14 8NS.

Home and School Council, 81 Rustlings Road, Sheffield S11 7AB.

Invalid Children's Aid Association, 126 Buckingham Palace Road, London SW1 9SB.

Joint Council for the Education of Handicapped Children, 4 Old Croft Road, Walton-on-the-Hill, Stafford ST17 0LS.

National Association for the Education of the Partially Sighted, The East Anglian School, Church road, Gt Yarmouth NR31 6LP.

National Association for Mental Health, 22 Harley Street, London W1N 2ED.

National Association for Remedial Education, 77 Chignal Road, Chelmsford CM1 2JA.

National Association of Teachers of the Mentally Handicapped, 1 Beechfield Avenue, Urmston, Manchester M31 3RT.

National Children's Bureau, 8 Wakley Street, London EC1.

National Confederation of Parent-Teacher Associations, 1 White Avenue, Northfleet, Gravesend, Kent.

National Council for Special Education, 1 Wood Street, Stratford-upon-Avon CV37 6JE.

National Foundation for Educational Research in England and Wales, The Mere, Upton Park, Slough, Berks SL1 2DQ.

National Deaf Children's Society, 31 Gloucester Place, London W1H 2EA.

National Elfrida Rathbone Society, 11a Whitworth Street, Manchester 1.

National Federation of Gateway Clubs, 17 Pembridge Square, London W2 4EP.

National Library for the Blind, Cromwell Road, Bredbury, Stockport SK6 2SG

National Society for Autistic Children, 1a Golders Green Road, London NW11 8EA.

National Society for Mentally Handicapped Children, 17 Pembridge Square, London W2 4EP.

Northern Ireland Council for Educational Research, 52 Malone Road, Belfast BT9 5BS.

Royal National Institute for the Blind, 224 Great Portland Street, London W1N 6AA.

Royal National Institute for the Deaf, 105 Gower Street, London WC1E 6AH.

Scottish Council for Research in Education, 16 Moray Place, Edinburgh EH3 6DR.

Scottish Council for Spastics, 22 Corstorphine Road, Edinburgh EH12 6HP.

Scottish Information Service for the Disabled, 18 Claremont Crescent, Edinburgh EH7 4QD.

Spastics Society, 12 Park Crescent, London W1N 4EQ.

Talking Books for the Handicapped, 49 Gt Cumberland Place, London W1H 7LH.

The Schools Council, 160 Great Portland Street, London W1N 6LL.

Toy Libraries Association, Seabrook House, Wyllyotts Manor, Darkes Lane, Potters Bar, Herts EN6 2HL.

Voluntary Council for Handicapped Children, 8 Wakley Street, London WC1V 7QE.

Youth Service Information Centre, (now the National Youth Bureau), 17-23 Albion Street, Leicester LE1 6GD.

Local Information

Addresses may be found in the telephone directory:
    Social Services department of the local authority
    The Local Education Office
    Citizens Advice Bureau
    Local office of the Department of Health and Social Security

FURTHER READING

There are few books which cover legislation and administration in special education. Pritchard's book and Chapter 2 of the Warnock Report offer the best brief accounts. For those who want more detail a source book is G. Taylor & J.B. Saunders, *The Law of Education*, Butterworth, though the 1976 edition does not cover recent Education Acts. Later editions will cover the points discussed in this book.

Recent general surveys of special education and the teaching of pupils with special educational needs are: Gulliford, R, *Special Educational Needs*, Routledge & Kegan Paul, 1971; Younghusband *et al, Living with Handicap*, National Bureau for Co-operation in Child Card, 1970; Ferneaux, B. *The Special Child*, Penguin, 1969. Jackson, S, *Special Education in England and Wales*, OUP 1966, and Segal, S.S., *No Child is Ineducable*, Pergamon, 1967 also cover the sweep of special education.

The proceedings of the First International Conference of The Association for Special Education, 1966, are published as *What Is Special Education?* and contributions by different authors cover content, organization, care and education of handicapped children, in the UK and abroad.

Services for Handicapped Youth in England and Wales, W.W. & I.W. Taylor, International Society for Rehabilitation of the Disabled, 1966, is a comprehensive technical document which has the advantage of being written by authors not involved in the system of special education which they describe.

The Psychological Assessment of Mental and Physical Handicaps, Part Two, Methuen, 1970, edited by Peter Mittler, is a book for those who wish to examine the professional aspects of assessment in depth.

The main educational journal covering special education is; *Special Education*, the journal of The National Council for Special Education. *Remedial Education*, which is the journal of The National Association for Remedial Education, covers work in ordinary schools.

Specially prepared for parents is the *Handbook for Parents with a Handicapped Child*, J. Stone & T. Taylor, Arrow, 1977. Also very useful is the *Directory for the Disabled* by A. Darnborough and D. Kinrade, published by Woodhead-Faulkner, in association with the Royal Association for Disability and Rehabilitation, 1977.

A recent significant addition to the literature is *Some of our Children*, M. Chazan, A.F. Laing, M. Shackleton-Bailey, and G. Jones, Open Books, 1980, and this concentrates, as its subtitle suggests on "the early education of children with special needs".

INDEX

Psychiatric Social Worker 26, 37
psychiatrists, role in assessment 26, 37
psychotherapists 4, 27, 37

reassessment (reviews of assessment)
  12, 18, 36, 52, 55, 58, 79
religious instruction 40
remedial teachers 27, 49, 77
*Report of the Committee of Enquiry
  into the Education of Handicapped
  Children and Young People, see*
  Warnock Report
retarded children, *see* Educationally
  Subnormal, learning difficulties
reviews, of assessment, *see* reassessment
Robert 5
rural areas, problems of 90—1

sanctuaries (in secondary schools) 15
School Meals Service 91
School Medical Service 24, 31—2, 34
School Psychological Service 67
School Report (in assessment) 34
School Welfare Service 24, 48, 66
schools
  ordinary:
    disabled educated in 12, 15—16,
    25—6, 40—2, 44, 47, 49, 58,
    63, 76—9, 84, (*see also* desig-
    nated units);
    staff problems 50, 66, 77;
    advice available to 64—5, 68;
    fall in population predicted 90;
    interaction with special schools
    93—6, 100, 109,
    see also boarding schools,
    comprehensive schools, hospital
    schools, independent schools,
    middle schools, primary schools,
    secondary schools
  special:
    attendance figures 12, 14, 16;
    history of development 39—40;
    disadvantages of 43—4;
    placement in 44—51, 76—9;
    staff problems 46, 92—4;
    effect of 1981 Education Act

on 58—9, 68, 90—1, 105—6,
    advice service for 64—5;
    curriculum development 68, 86,
    89, 91—2, 96—8, 100;
    interaction with ordinary
    schools 93—6, 100, 109;
    see also, teachers, training of
Schools Council Project 42
secondary schools:
  sanctuaries in 15,
  reorganization of 43,
  designated units in 77, 100
Secretary of State for Education:
  powers of 28, 55, 72, 73, 75;
  duties of 40,
  parents' right of appeal to 105
signing systems (for the deaf) 7
sixth forms 98
slow learners, *see* Educationally
  Subnormal, learning difficulties
Social Report 34
social services, support of handicapped children 3, 12, 29, 60—1,
  73
social workers, assistance available
  from 21, 37, 84
special education:
  goals of 11;
  organization and finance 14—15;
  at pre-school level 29—30, 82—4;
  legal requirement to provide 36;
  range of provision required 51—2,
  88—9;
  regional organization of 64, 95;
  curriculum development 68, 86,
  89, 91—2, 96—8, 100;
  placement of children in 44—51,
  76—9;
  quality of 82;
  see also assessment, teachers, training of
Special Education (journal) 106, 109
special educational needs:
  concept of 2, 54—7, 58;
  temporary 57, 58;
  see also assessment
Special Educational Needs (DES,
  1978), *see* Warnock Report

Special Educational Treatment (SET)
40, 77
Special Needs in Education (White
Paper 1980) 54, 55, 79
special schools, *see* schools, special
speech defects (language disorders)
13, 16
speech therapists 73, 82
spina bifida 14
'statements' of special educational
needs 54–7, 66–7, 70, 74, 77, 86,
99, 104–5;
see also assessment
Statutory Instrument 40
Susan 9, 10

teachers:
in ordinary schools:
role in identification of children
with special needs 2, 17, 25–6,
32, 37, 73;
in-service training for 23, 65,
80, 84, 89, 104
in special education:

training of 25, 42, 60–1, 62,
64, 77, 99, 106;
in designated units 87, 90;
motivation of 92;
interaction with ordinary
schools 94;
see also peripatetic teachers
toy libraries 68, 83
training centres 98

unemployment, of disabled 97

vocational guidance 97–8
voluntary societies 21, 37, 60, 69, 80,
83–4, 99

Warnock Report *(Special Educational
Needs*, DES, 1978) 13, 51, 54–6,
56–7, 59–61, 64, 66, 70, 72, 81,
85, 90, 93, 101, 109;
priorities of 103–4;
compared to 1981 Education Act
106–7

ABBREVIATIONS

A&SS   Advisory and Support Service
AEO/SE   Assistant Education Officer for Special Education
DES   Department of Education and Science
ESN   Educationally Subnormal
EWO   Educational Welfare Officer
FE   Further Education
ILEA   Inner London Education Authority
JCC   Joint Consultative Committee
LEA   Local Education Authority
PSW   Psychiatric Social Worker
SE   Special Education
SET   Special Educational Treatment
SMO   School Medical Officer